Liverpool b

LIVER POOL
FOOTBALL CLUB

Liverpool Football Club

Stan Liversedge

Vantage Books

Distributed by Robert Hale Limited

First published in Great Britain 1976 by
Vantage Books in conjunction with
Elmswood Publications, Liverpool

Layout by John Leach

Distributed by
Robert Hale Limited
Clerkenwell House
Clerkenwell Green
London EC1R OHT

ISBN 0 904545 05 9 (Hardcover)
ISBN 0 904545 06 7 (Paperback)

Filmset by Specialised Offset Services Limited, Liverpool
and printed and bound in Great Britain by
Redwood Burn Limited, Trowbridge & Esher

ACKNOWLEDGMENTS

The Author and Publishers are grateful to the Liverpool Daily Post and Echo, the Sunday People and Harry Ormesher for permission to reproduce photographs.

A pile driver from Roger Hunt

Contents

1 '... Liverpool has become almost a religion'

When you have supported the same team for fifty years, you form an attachment to the club whose colours they wear. The names and the faces may change, but your heart remains with that club. Liverpool Football Club's chairman, John W. Smith, confesses that half a century of association with the Anfield club has only served to make the bonds even tighter. 'For me, Liverpool has become almost a religion,' he says simply.

That makes Liverpool's chairman something more than an official of the club: it identifies him immediately as a Liverpool fan, and, indeed, he admits to having played truant from school more than once, to get a glimpse of his idols on the Soccer field at Anfield. His father was a shareholder of the club, and he saw his first Liverpool match when he was a four-year-old.

'I can recall when the gates used to be opened about fifteen minutes from the end of the match, and that's when the youngsters would get in free. My father used to remark that the "shareholders" were arriving, when he saw the influx of schoolboys. I didn't even begin to suspect then that, one day, I would become the chairman of such a famous club.'

John Smith had a favourite player, of course – the great Elisha Scott, an Irishman. 'The finest goalkeeper I ever saw – and we've had some great ones,' he says. 'I remember one occasion when Liverpool were playing Everton, and Dixie Dean was their centre-forward ... that day, Scott took a real tumble, because Dean scored a goal when he bundled Scott and the ball into the net. The goalkeeper wasn't given the protection he is today, of course.'

John Smith remembers 'Parson' Jackson, too, a full-back who saved his pay because it could contribute toward his studies for the Ministry. 'Scott had a rich command of choice words, and "Parson" Jackson used to remonstrate with the Irishman ... to no avail.' Jackson, just one of the men who served Liverpool so well, did eventually become a parson.

What does John Smith remember about local derby games? 'They were outstanding occasions, as they are now. It used to give me a tremendous feeling when I saw the two teams – Liverpool and Everton – come out on the field together. There were a great number of personalities in the sides.'

International Caps are presented to Cyril Sidlow and Ray Lambert after a match at Anfield in October 1947.

'I sometimes feel that Liverpool became Merseyside's counterpart of Manchester United. At one time, it seemed that Everton and Manchester City reigned supreme in their respective cities. Then we saw the emergence of Manchester United from the doldrums, and in the same way, after an indifferent spell during the 1920s and 1930s, Liverpool became giants on Merseyside.'

One of the old-time stars who wore the colours of Liverpool was a left-winger called Fred Hopkin. He was known by the nickname of 'Polly', and it was generally acknowledged that he was a maker of goals. In fact, no one expected him to score them. 'But one day, "Polly" Hopkin did score a goal – and suddenly, as the crowd roared its delight, you realised that the old Kemlyn Road stand was on fire! I don't know exactly how it happened, but I do remember the fire engine arriving ...'

Hopkin used to supply an inside-forward called Harry 'Smiler' Chambers with the scoring ammunition. Eventually, of course, time took its toll, and Chambers moved on from Anfield to West Bromich. By that time, too, Elisha

Scott could not command a regular first-team place at Liverpool. John Smith, who went to second-team games as well as the big matches, remembers seeing both players in action in a reserve game at Anfield.

Scott was succeeded in the first team by a South African named Arthur Riley, who was just one of several Springbok footballers who became Liverpool players. Others were Gordon Hodgson, Berry Nieuwenhuys and Bob Priday. John Smith says: 'We had very close commercial ties with South Africa, and with the football authorities over there, and when the South Africans sent over a touring side in 1924, the ball started rolling. Hodgson and Riley were both members of that side – Hodgson became a fast bowler with Lancashire, as well as a famous footballer with Liverpool. He went on to Leeds and Aston Villa, and then became manager of Port Vale.'

A view of the new Players Lounge opened at Anfield in the autumn of 1971 with Bob Paisley and Bill Shankly in the foreground.

The new stand at Anfield opened for the 1972-3 season.

Hodgson, of course, won fame as a scorer of goals – later Billy Liddell and Roger Hunt became the scoring heroes at Anfield – and when Liverpool's chairman gets around to the subject of goals, he remembers a local derby game in which Liverpool beat Everton 7-4. 'That was one of the finest derby matches I remember – it was the day Harold "Boy" Barton scored either three or four of our goals.'

Anfield, as Liverpool's chairman says, has had its heroes from Scotland, Ireland and Wales, as well as South Africa. There have always been men who seemed larger than life, as they figured in Liverpool's achievements. The chairman is proud of the Liverpool supporters, too. 'Anfield has always been a ground with a family atmosphere, because the spectators are close to the pitch and they are able to feel more involved with the game and the players than at many other grounds. This closeness has given our supporters the feeling that they are part and parcel of the club ... as, indeed, is the case.'

'Liverpool ARE a great club. We have a fine record, in so many ways, and I am always somewhat surprised and delighted to discover, when we travel abroad, how much our name means to people who can never even get to a match at Anfield. Just as Manchester United became the toast of Europe [as successors to Real Madrid], so I believe that Liverpool will become the acknowledged kings of Continental football. We are well on the way to that kind of reputation now, with thirteen successive seasons in Europe to our credit.'

John Smith believes, too, that the teamwork off the field plays just as important a part, and always has done, as the teamwork on it. He makes the point firmly: 'What happened, when Bill Shankly – without doubt, one of the real giants of the game – decided to retire as manager of Liverpool? Other clubs have had problems galore, when it came to appointing managers ... we decided that the thing to do was to keep it in the family, and so we handed Bob Paisley the job.'

'Bob's accent may not be Merseyside, but he is as Scouse as they come in his regard for this club. And we didn't bring in one man from outside – we promoted Joe Fagan, Ronnie Moran and Roy Evans, and so we maintained

Seventeen players, pictured in the Liverpool squad of the 1960s . . . and now, only half a dozen of them are still at Anfield. On the back row (left to right): Geoff Strong, Gerry Byrne, Chris Lawler, Tommy Lawrence, Ray Clemence, Larry Lloyd, Ian Ross, Alec Lindsay. Front row: Ian Callaghan, Alun Evans, Roger Hunt, Tommy Smith, Ron Yeats, Emlyn Hughes, Ian St. John, Peter Thompson, Bobby Graham. Now, only Clemence, Lindsay, Callaghan, Smith and Hughes remain.

Bill Shankly and twenty-one first team squad players. Back row (left to right): Steve Heighway, Alec Lindsay, Tommy Lawrence, Ray Clemence, Chris Lawler, Phil Boersma. Centre row: Brian Hall, Roy Evans, John McLaughlin, Emlyn Hughes, Larry Lloyd, Ron Yeats, John Toshack, Ian Ross, Jack Whitham. Front row: Bobby Graham, Alun Evans, Tommy Smith, Bill Shankly, Ian Callaghan, Peter Thompson, Kevin Keegan.

the family feeling and the continuity. Right through the years, our club has had players who have stayed to serve in other capacities, once their playing days were over.'

The chairman recalls, too, that breweries have taken a benevolent interest in the footballing affairs of Liverpool. Right at the start there was John Houlding, a former Lord Mayor of the city, who played a major role in the birth of the club. 'He was one of our original supporters, and he was a brewer with premises in Breck Road. He owned some public-houses, including the *Sandon*, which is just a few hundred yards from Anfield.

'In fact, there was a time when players used to change at the *Sandon* and then walk across to the Kop. And there is a Houlding Street close to the ground. John Houlding sold his business interests in the early 1930s to another brewery. And, by a coincidence, the chairman of Liverpool FC today is a director of a brewery.'

Liverpool's chairman pays a glowing tribute to the late Mr T.V. Williams, who devoted his whole life to the club. He will be remembered for many things, not least the fact that he played a major role in taking Bill Shankly to Anfield; but John Smith believes the act which 'T.V.' would have rated as possibly his greatest achievement was the building of Liverpool's magnificent

Liverpool player and University graduate Brian Hall seen during training at Anfield.

training headquarters at Melwood. 'T.V. Williams was instrumental in purchasing nine or ten acres of land, and that was how Melwood came into being. I believe that this was one of the best things he did for the club – and he did a great deal for Liverpool, in other ways.'

Mr Williams' recollections of games at Anfield went back even more than half a century, and John Smith says: 'I remember chatting with "T.V." one day, not so long ago, and he was telling me about an occasion in season 1905-6, when Liverpool won the Championship.

'That day, "T.V." – after having scored eight goals for this school team in the morning – sat, as usual, on the dressing-room bench at the corner of Anfield Road and Kemlyn Road. The Press sent the details of the game by pigeon ... and that was the day when the Kop [only one-third of its present size] started to sing the famous songs which have gone round the world.'

There is a personal recollection which Liverpool's present chairman savours, too. These days, Soccer stars often have their own individual traits – Rodney Marsh, for instance, during his years in English soccer, did not wear shin-guards and liked to play with his stockings rolled down – and one of Liverpool's heroes of the past was also easily identifiable. He was Tommy Bromilow – 'the first player I ever saw who played with his shirt outside his shorts,' says John Smith.

For Liverpool, of course, it is the present and the future that matter most; in recent years, they have not concentrated solely on producing a great First Division side. They showed great foresight in the appointment of a former schoolmaster, Tom Saunders, as their youth-development officer, and this man, with such close knowledge of schoolboy Soccer (he was the England boys' team manager), is guiding youngsters on the right lines as they develop into players of great promise. Augmenting this youth scheme is chief scout Geoff Twentyman, a former Liverpool player, who travels thousands of miles each year, watching and assessing talent which might be suitable for Liverpool.

So behind the team is another team, strong and united, as Liverpool's chairman says. His devotion to the club speaks for itself: 'I still get the same thrill out of seeing the Liverpool players go on the field that I did when I was a boy. Whenever the players emerge from the tunnel, my mind goes back to the days when I was a lad, and I felt so proud to be a Liverpool supporter. And I still am.'

Kevin Keegan during training at Anfield.

2 These were the Liverpool Lads

So far as the modern generation of football spectators is concerned, Liverpool's history probably began in December, 1959, when Bill Shankly, a man who has become a legend in his own lifetime, and the idol of the Kop, arrived at Anfield as the team's new manager. Doubtless, too, the Liverpool faithful have an unswerving belief that the story of Liverpool's success started by Shankly and carried on by Bob Paisley will last for ever and ever.

What the future will bring, no one can foretell with real certainty, of course, though it does seem likely that Liverpool will remain among the giants of football for a long time to come. But even though it may seem like heresy, Liverpool Football Club had a history, a heartbeat and a fervour, a record of achievement all its own before the Shankly era. The story of Liverpool Football Club really began close on a century ago. There is plenty of evidence that people were sufficiently stirred to show their depth of feeling about it, even in the distant past.

The story of the Liverpool Club is long and tortuous and can be traced back to the founding in the nineteenth century of the St Domingo FC. Then the name of this club was changed to Everton FC and, believe it or not, gate money of thirteen shillings (65p) was once taken when the team played a game in the Priory Road ground. It was 1878 when St Domingo came into existence, and 1884 when Everton FC, as they had become known, made Anfield Road their home ground. But in 1892 a dispute between the club and the owner of the ground led to Everton FC moving to Goodison Park. That year a new club, Liverpool FC, took over Anfield.

Liverpool joined the Lancashire League, won the Championship at their first attempt, and, having won it, found themselves having to pay £127 to replace the trophy, which they discovered they had somehow lost. This, then, is how it all began, the story of a club which, as the years passed, gained a tremendous hold upon the affections of half a city. And that does not take into account the support of the thousands of Liverpool fanatics throughout the world.

To a considerable degree, the story of Liverpool Football Club is bound up with that of the Liverpool Boys football team, for many of the youngsters born and bred in the city achieved their ambition to play football for Liverpool after playing for the boys team. Players who had graduated through the schoolboy sides became glittering stars with the Anfield club. In 1907, when Everton were finalists in the FA Cup, the brothers Billy and Bob Balmer were full-back partners; and forty years later, when Liverpool won the Championship of the First Division, it was their nephew, Jackie, who was the Reds' skipper, and he totalled ten goals in three successive matches. Such is the thread which runs through the footballing story of a city where even closely-knit families can be split by loyalty to one or other of the Big Two, Liverpool and Everton.

Eddie Spicer photographed when he had been selected to play for the England boys team in 1937.

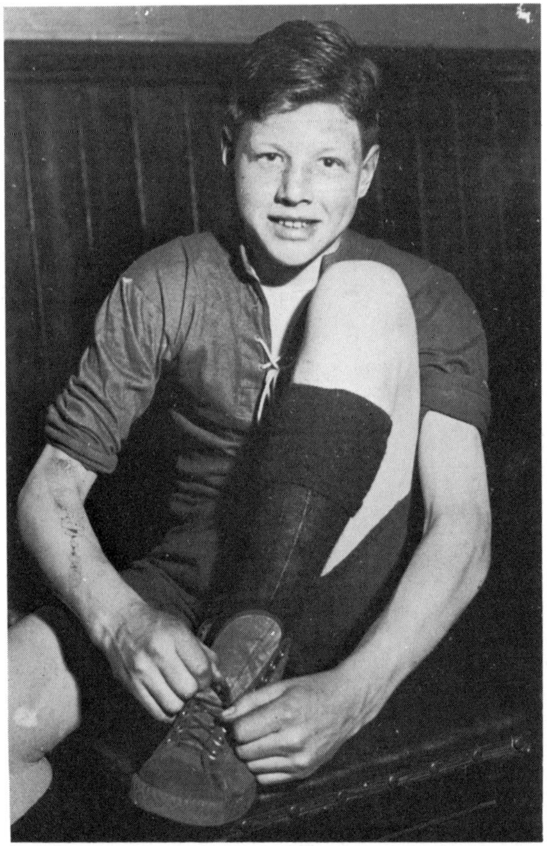

One of the Liverpool Boys of more than sixty years ago was called Tommy Bromilow. He captained Fonthill Road School, and in season 1919-20 he presented himself one day at the doors of Anfield, football boots tucked under his arm, and asked for a trial. He stayed to become a member of the Liverpool teams which won the First Division Championship in 1921-2-3. Tommy, capped five times for England, missed only one of eighty-four games: his brother, Bill, was for a long time a goal-keeper with Everton.

The past decade has provided something of a parallel with the story of Tomy Bromilow, for no fewer than three Liverpool lads – Ian Callaghan, Tommy Smith and Chris Lawler – arrived at Anfield and made their mark by achieving not only almost all the honours available, but by contributing to the success of Liverpool by being consistently selected as members of the team. Between them, in just over ten years, these three modern heroes of Merseyside Soccer have totalled more than 1,700 games. Lawler has now moved on, but his contribution to the cause of Liverpool will long be remembered.

Further back in Liverpool's history – but still remembered by the older generation who saw them in action – there were Eddie Spicer and Laurie Hughes. Spicer captained the Liverpool city team and won schoolboy International honours against Scotland and Ireland before entering into professional football as a player with Liverpool. He was a member of the 1946-7 side which took the First Division Championship, and he played in the 1950 FA Cup final, which Liverpool lost, 2-0, against Arsenal. Sadly, Spicer had his career curtailed by injury.

Laurie Hughes played in the 1937-8 Liverpool Boys team, and he was to become an automatic choice as Liverpool's centre-half for many years. He played alongside Spicer in the 1946-7 Championship team, and in the 1950 Wembley final. In the World Cup year of 1950 Hughes also played for England.

The years of the Second World War did not prevent the Liverpool Boys under-15 side achieving success, and in 1940 this team gained two trophies. They won four games, drew the fifth, and scored 21 goals against 5. In that team was a youngster called Les Shannon who was to become a Liverpool player. The crop of local youngsters continued with names like Jimmy Melia and Gerry Byrne. Both these players were to win England International Caps, and Byrne was to become a hero in the 1965 FA Cup final at Wembley, when he played on, despite a broken collar bone, and collected a winner's medal. The Liverpool Boys team of season 1952-3 was coloured a great deal by the influence and prestige of Melia, for the player from St Anthony's school became the first to play for England Boys and for the full England team.

For more than thirty-five years a Soccer enthusiast named Harold Williams had a close association with the schoolboy footballers; at different times he was selector, team manager, treasurer and chairman of the Liverpool Schools Football Association. One of his outstanding recollections is of a day in 1952, when forty-four players from all over the city had been selected for final trials. They were the pick of the bunch – and Melia was among them. So was a lad named Johnny King, who later became a professional with Tranmere Rovers.

Harold recalls how, when the trial was over, a colleague asked him: 'Well, how many do you reckon you've got into the team?'

Harold's answer: 'One and a half, I should say.' He went on to explain: 'There's a little, black-haired fellow [Melia, of St Anthony's] who keeps shooting at goal, and another tiny fellow [King, of Gilmour] who never gives him a moment's peace, and keeps cutting him off at the ankles!'

Only a few weeks later, before Melia had been chosen to play for Lancashire Boys and England Boys, a quietly spoken scout was inquiring if anyone had shown interest in the Liverpool lad. The scout himself had no reservations about Melia's ability, or his future in professional football, but he learned that he might as well forget about the chances of signing him for his club. His hopes were nil – for that club, Walsall, was at the time holding up the rest of the footballing world – at the bottom of the old Third Division (South).

Another photograph of Eddie Spicer whose career was cut short by injury.

In the 1952-3 season, Melia scored 27 goals as a member of the Liverpool Boys team, and he went on to achieve a fine reputation as a professional player with Liverpool, before moving on to Wolves and then Southampton.

As for Gerry Byrne, a remarkable fact about his career is that, though he was to win fame as a member of Bill Shankly's great side of the 1960s, he never played in one competitive game for the Liverpool Boys side, even though he was a member of the first team squad. Today, on Merseyside, Gerry is still the hero who played for 115 minutes with that broken collar bone, and kept the secret until Liverpool had finally triumphed against Leeds with an extra-time goal in the 1965 final. This was the player of whom Shankly said, 'When Gerry had to hang up his boots, it took a big chunk out of Liverpool. Somehow, something was missing ... .'

However, the day of retirement was far, far away when Melia and Byrne teamed up together to play for England against Scotland at Wembley. The date was 6 April, 1963. Melia, who made his debut for Liverpool as a seventeen-year-old, played an outstanding part in their long-overdue return to the First Division, and when he left for Wolves, in 1964, after ten seasons at Anfield, he had scored 79 goals in 268 appearances. As Wolves paid a £50 000 fee for him, it was clear that Liverpool had had tremendous service from Melia. Although his travels took him to Aldershot, as well as Molineux and The Dell, before he became manager at Crewe, Melia, who later moved into soccer abroad, remains very much a Liverpool lad at heart. The accent is still unchanged, and Merseyside, for him, is still home.

Byrne was another modest, quietly spoken player; a pleasant chap who had a slow but engaging smile. He was signed for the Anfield club along with Melia, in 1953. In time, his name went on the transfer list – but Bill Shankly made sure it did not stay there. Gerry blossomed as a full-back whom all opponents respected. He won England Under-23 honours and went on to gain full International Caps. With Liverpool, he collected League Championship medals in 1964 and 1966; and, of course, he had an FA Cup-winner's medal, to make up the hat-trick, after that gallant performance in the Wembley battle against Leeds. And, just in case it is forgotten, he was also a member of England's victorious World Cup squad in 1966.

Melia and Byrne are but two of the players who helped to compose Liverpool's history on the field of play. There were other heroes before them, there have been other heroes since, and, doubtless, there will be still more

Laurie Hughes who played in the 1937-8 Liverpool boys team and went on to become the regular Centre-half at Anfield.

heroes when the present idols of Anfield have disappeared from the scene. When Liverpool first took over at Anfield, paying an annual rent of £100, few people had visions of the history that was to be made, with stirring deeds in abundance on a ground where Liverpool themselves were to become regarded as virtually invincible. The ground, later bought outright, has been developed into one of the finest in the country. The first Liverpool League game there, on 9 September, 1893, produced a gate of 5000 for the battle against Lincoln; today, when clubs such as Leeds and Everton are the visitors, Anfield stages a guaranteed 55,000 full house.

Gerry Byrne, Ian Callaghan and Gordon Milne, members of the 1966 England World Cup squad and all Liverpool players.

England Manager Alf Ramsey talking to Gerry Byrne, Gordon Milne and Jimmy Melia, all Liverpool players and members of the England squad in 1963.

Anfield, incidentally, has played its part in the story of the Liverpool Boys team, for it was there, on Whit Monday, 1948, that a record attendance of more than 40 000 saw Liverpool Boys competing in the final of the English Schools Trophy, and sharing the trophy with Stockport. Season 1975-6 saw the current Liverpool Boys side score an overall 4-3 victory in the two-legged final against Slough, and take the English Schools Trophy, to make the spring of 1976 an occasion for yet another celebration on Merseyside.

There were 37 500 people at Goodison when Liverpool Schools Football Association staged the 1954-5 England schoolboy International match against Scotland. The fact that the weather was depressing merely serves to emphasise how well Merseyside fans will support the game they follow with such fervour. That particular game ended in a 2-2 draw, and although there was plenty to admire in the football of both teams, one player drew more comment than most. He was a youngster called Johnny Morrissey, a local lad who was a product of St Sylvester's School, and who was then in his second season with the city team. He was to become one of the professionals who played for both Liverpool and Everton. He served Liverpool from 1957 to 1962, then cost Everton a £10 000 fee, and went on to win two Championship medals, an FA Cup-finalist's medal, and representative honours with the Football League.

He was just one more of the local lads who made good on Merseyside, and, as has been said, there were many of them. One player of the mid-1950s did leave Anfield after a relatively short stay, and for a give-away fee. He was Willie Carlin, who later made a name with Derby County, Sheffield United and Leicester, among other clubs. A contemporary of Carlin's was also to join Liverpool – and he is still there. Ian Callaghan, Footballer of the Year at the end of season 1973-74, holder of the club record for appearances, and, at the time of his schoolboy Soccer exploits, a diminutive wing-half. He was to become a winger whom defenders feared and an England International, before reverting to the wing-half role which nowadays is dubbed 'midfield.'

Callaghan joined Liverpool as an amateur, and signed as a professional in 1960. He won England youth and under-23 honours, and a place in England's 1966 World Cup squad. He was a member of the Liverpool team which won promotion in 1962, collected Championship medals in 1964 and 1966, and completed these honours with an FA Cup-winner's medal. More recently, he went to Wembley again and finished on the losing side against Arsenal, picked up another Championship medal and a UEFA Cup-winner's medal, and returned to Wembley for a winner's medal in the spring of 1974.

In the spring of 1976, he was there again, as Liverpool, for the second time in four years, carried off the League Championship and the UEFA Cup. Callaghan made his debut for Liverpool as an eighteen-year-old, replacing the great Billy Liddell; few realised then that he would beat Liddell's 532-match record of appearances for Liverpool, and play more than 750 games for his one and only club.

If you recall Callaghan, you must also think of those other two contemporaries, Tommy Smith and Chris Lawler, who once played together in the 1959 Liverpool Boys team, and were destined to play hundreds of games alongside each other in the colours of Liverpool.

In 1957 the Southport Schools Football Association invited a Liverpool under-13 team to play the home boys at Haig Avenue. The Liverpool officials

Leslie Shannon, Liverpool Boys team and Anfield player who later was transferred to Burnley.

Johnny Morrissey, a local Liverpool boy, who played for Liverpool from 1957 to 1962 and was then transferred to Everton.

selected a tall, slim, poker-faced thirteen-year-old as captain of their side. He was an immaculate ball player who carried out his pre-match instructions flawlessly. His name was Chris Lawler, and when the game was over, Liverpool's officials reckoned that they had seen England's future centre-half in action that day.

Lawler did become the England Boys centre-half, and he was their skipper in the six games they played during the 1958-9 season. He also went on to play for the full England International team, but at full-back, the position he made his own for so long at Liverpool, though he did play for Liverpool at centre-half, on occasion.

The quiet man of Anfield, he signed for Liverpool in 1959 and won England youth, Under-23 and, finally, full International Status, and also played at centre-half for the Football League. He maintained a remarkable record of consistency by playing hundreds of games for his club without once being out through injury. He also carved himself a special niche as a full-back who could score goals – more than sixty of them, and not one from the penalty spot. And, like Callaghan and Smith, he collected a great number of medals.

Ironically, Lawler finally dropped out of the Liverpool team mid-way through the 1973-4 season and provided a new lease of life for his team-mate and friend, Tommy Smith, who had been in the shadows for a spell because of the changed policy at Anfield. It was Smith who slotted into the No. 2 position, and he kept Lawler out when the latter was fit again. Then, in season 1974-5, when the emerging young star Phil Thompson was a victim of cartilage damage, Lawler and Smith played side by side once more, as they had done so many times before. By the end of season 1975-6, Lawler had moved on to Portsmouth, but Smith had claimed the No. 2 jersey, to win renewed admiration for his displays.

Smith, one-time skipper at Liverpool, and for years automatically the wearer of the No. 4 jersey, was born to play for the club, it was said. He was regarded as a hard defensive player by most people, and few would deny that he possessed rugged qualities. But there was an occasion when Bill Shankly was moved to say of him: 'The way he has been playing, it will be a disgrace to football if he doesn't collect at least one International Cap, before he finishes. He's not just a hard man – he's got a tremendous amount of ability.'

Smith duly did collect an International Cap with England, to join Liverpool's swelling ranks of Internationals – in fact, counting the Scots, the

Irish and the Welsh, they could field a complete team of Internationals by the start of season 1974-5. Shankly's words about Smith's ability were completely justified when he took on the No. 2 job and calmly proceeded to cut down to size many a winger who, as the cynics had forecast, would 'skin' him. Smith did not do this crudely, either: he used skill and his footballing brain to do the job effectively.

As a boy, Chris Lawler played for St Teresa's, while Tommy Smith was a pupil at the Archbishop Godfrey school. With Ian Callaghan, these two formed the cornerstone of the rebuilt Liverpool side, after the great team of the 1960s was broken up. Smith's father was a fervent supporter of the Reds, and he wanted his lad to play for Liverpool. Unhappily, his father did not live to see that proud day: it was his mother who took her son to see Bill Shankly, and now the rest is history. There is an interesting sidelight on Tommy Smith, though, which shows his characteristic readiness to stand up for what he considers to be his right. The incident happened back in 1958, when he played for Archbishop Godfrey in a Cup-tie against Anfield Road. Those were the days before substitutes were allowed, and even then, as now, Tommy Smith knew what he was about. He obviously had even then the professional instinct which has stood him in such good stead through the years since 1958.

During the first half a player in the Anfield Road team injured a foot, and at the interval, after some discussion between the masters, it was agreed that a replacement should be allowed. As the reserve player was getting changed, up strode the Archbishop Godfrey skipper to tell one of the masters: 'Excuse me, sir, but you can't do that – substitutes aren't allowed.' The master had to admit that this was indeed the case, and so Tommy Smith had both made and won his point. The reserve retired from the scene, and the injured lad took his place once more in the Anfield Road line-up. Perhaps Tommy later wished he had said nothing, because Anfield Road managed to win the tie!

Perhaps, though, it was Smith's own attitude towards the game that prompted him in part to make his protest, for he has neither asked nor given quarter during his professional career, being ready always to accept the knocks. When he goes down and stays down, as opponents will readily admit, then you know he has really been hurt. Smith has now played more than 550 games for Liverpool and, like Lawler and Callaghan, he has collected his share of the medals. He, too, graduated to full England status via youth and Under-23 selections.

Tommy Smith at home with his wife Susan and children Darren and Janette.

Local Liverpool stalwarts Ian Callaghan, Chris Lawler and Tommy Smith.

3 The last line... and the firing line

From the late 1890s, to the present day, the history of Liverpool has taken some unexpected turnings, and so many players have made their mark. Liverpool's telegraphic address is 'Goalkeeper', and, most fittingly, they have produced some outstanding men as their last line of defence. The great Elisha Scott held sway for many years; there was Arthur Riley, the South African, Doug Rudham, Welsh International Cyril Sidlow, Scottish Internationals Tommy Younger and Tommy Lawrence, and now, fit to rank with the best, Ray Clemence who has become an England International.

Some goalkeepers have stayed a comparatively short time, others were Liverpool players for many years – but all made their mark, as characters and 'keepers who could save goals. Even during the Second World War, when players guested for different clubs, Liverpool were not to be outdone: for at various times they were able to call on the services of Frank Swift and Sam Bartram as guest players.

Chesterfield are another club who have earned a reputation for producing goalkeepers – one immediately thinks of Gordon Banks who, it must be said, became a great favourite with the Anfield supporters, even though he so often produced brilliant saves against Liverpool. It was from Chesterfield, too, that Sam Hardy came, to join the Anfield club and be hailed as one of the greatest 'keepers football had known. He joined Liverpool in 1905, and his first season with them saw him win a Championship medal. By the time he moved on to Aston Villa, in 1912, he had played 218 League games for Liverpool, and won 14 of his 21 England Caps with the Anfield club. He retained an affection for Liverpool even after his departure, and no one was more delighted than Hardy when they won the FA Cup for the first time, in 1965. Happy that he had lived to see this happen, he died a few months later, at the age of seventy-nine.

If Hardy was an England international, Elisha Scott – whose brother, William, played for Everton – became a legendary figure as goalkeeper for Liverpool and Ireland, with whom he won 31 International Caps. Scott set a club record of 428 League appearances, between 1912 and 1934. That record

South African goal keeper Doug Rudhan who made twenty-five appearances in League and Cup matches before turning professional at Anfield in the mid-fifties.

was later overtaken by Billy Liddell and then by Ian Callaghan. The Irish have produced some fine 'keepers, through the years; one thinks of Harry Gregg, who was voted the world's No. 1 in the 1958 World Cup, and Pat Jennings, who has given Tottenham such superb service – but Scott was voted by many people to be the finest 'keeper ever to come out of Ireland.

Just after the First World War, when Liverpool captured the Championship in two successive seasons, Scott played in 81 of the 84 matches, and conceded only 63 goals. Later, Liverpool were to become noted for more defensive economy, as they surged through to collect honours in the era after the Second World War. And again, goalkeepers played no small part.

Liverpool have had men from England, Scotland, Ireland and Wales as their last line of defence, and it was a Scot, Kenny Campbell, who was their 'keeper in the FA Cup final of 1914. He arrived from Cambuslang in 1911, and served Liverpool for ten years, winning eight International Caps. It was to Scott that Campbell lost his place; he moved on to other clubs, finally returning to Merseyside to finish with New Brighton. Campbell remained a Liverpool man at heart, too, and he lived to see them return to Wembley in the early 1970s.

There have been South Africans, too, at Anfield – again, the name of players such as 'Nivvy' Nieuwenhuys, Bob Priday and company spring to mind. One of the Springbok clan was Doug Rudham, who became the last amateur to play for Liverpool. He made twenty-five appearances in League and Cup matches before turning professional at Anfield in the mid-1950s. But even before that, Liverpool had a goalkeeper who hailed from South Africa. His name was Arthur Riley, and he arrived after having played with the famous Gordon Hodgson (of whom more later) for the South African touring side of 1924. Riley at first was in the shadow of Elisha Scott, but when the Irishman stepped down, Riley came into his own. He stayed to play 323 League games in sixteen years, and was one of Liverpool's ever-dependables during the 1930s. Later, he worked on the Anfield ground staff, and was able to pass on valuable tips to players such as Cyril Sidlow, who himself became a Welsh International.

Sidlow, who began his playing career at Molineux, cost Liverpool £4000 when he was transferred to them in February, 1946, and he collected seven Welsh Caps during his career. He also played in Liverpool's 1950 FA Cup-

Tom Younger, Liverpool's Scottish International goal-keeper, slips a header over the bar during a match with Charlton in 1958.

Younger again tipping a shot over the bar during a match with Fulham in 1959.

Another Scottish goal-keeper at Anfield was Tommy Lawrence who played more than 370 games for Liverpool.

final team against Arsenal, and when he retired a year later, he was only one game short of 150 League appearances for the Anfield club. He would clearly have made many more, too, but the Second World War interrupted his career, for he served with the Royal Air Force.

So we come to the later generation of Liverpool goalkeepers. There was the amiable giant, Tommy Younger, who won sixteen of his twenty-four Scotland caps while a Liverpool player, and who missed only four senior games during something like four years at Anfield. In fact, Tommy Younger, who became a director of Hibernian, the club for whom he had previously played, proudly claims that he never played second-team football during his time at Liverpool. He cost Liverpool a then record fee of £13 000, and when he returned to Scotland, as player-manager of Falkirk, another 'keeper, Bert Slater, arrived at Anfield as part of the deal.

There was another Scot, another Tommy (but surnamed Lawrence). Tommy Lawrence has a Lancashire accent, despite his qualification for Scotland, and he was a man in the shadows for several years before he finally gained a regular first-team place. When he did so, he went on to collect three Scotland Caps and play more than 370 games for Liverpool. He was a member of the great Liverpool side of the 1960s which coasted through Championship, FA Cup and European campaigns.

And this, of course, brings us to the player who succeeded Lawrence in goal – Ray Clemence, signed from Scunthorpe for less than £20 000, and the club's first England International 'keeper since the days of Sam Hardy more than sixty years ago. Clemence, too, has proved a bargain since he joined Liverpool in 1967. Like Lawrence, he had to wait a considerable time to gain a first-team place, but when Bill Shankly finally began to make changes in his great side of the 1960s, Clemence arrived – to stay. He looks as if he will be an integral part of Liverpool's defence for years to come. When he did take over from Lawrence, he confirmed his place with more than 100 consecutive appearances, and he is now virtually ever-present.

However, if Liverpool have had some first-class goalkeepers, men whose job was to blot out the scoring efforts of opposing attackers, they have seldom been lacking firepower themselves, and the names of forwards who knew the shortest route to goal are strewn abundantly throughout the Liverpool story. Gordon Hodgson, Albert Stubbins, Billy Liddell, Roger Hunt, Ian St John, Kevin Keegan, John Toshack – these names spring swiftly to mind.

If illness had not cut short the life of George Allan, at the age of twenty-four, one wonders how much more impact he would have made on the scene at Anfield – and yet, during his brief spell there, he became a hero. He arrived from Leith in 1895, going into the side which captured the Second Division Championship; he became Liverpool's first Scottish International two years later, when he played against England as leader of the attack. He went back to Scotland to play for Celtic, then rejoined Liverpool, helping them finish as First Division runners-up in season 1898-9.

Not for the first time, Liverpool had a scoring centre-forward from the North-East when Albert Stubbins joined the Anfield club. He arrived from Newcastle – but something like forty years previously, a character called Joe Hewitt was signed from Sunderland, and when Liverpool carried off the League Championship in season 1905-6 it was Hewitt who did a great deal of the damage to opposing defences, for he scored 22 goals that season. Injury finished his career in 1910, but he stayed at Anfield, and when he finally retired, he had served sixty years with the club. This loyalty and long service had been a feature, indeed, in many cases where players have stayed to help forge Liverpool's history. Again and again former players have become backroom members of the Anfield team, and team-mamager Bob Paisley is today's outstanding example.

Another player who was a Geordie was Harry Chambers, who arrived at Anfield during the First World War and enjoyed a leading role in Liverpool's successive Championship seasons at the start of the 1920s. Chambers scored 22 goals in the 1921-2 Championship season, and 19 when Liverpool claimed the title again the following year. He had a tremendous understanding with another Geordie, left-winger Fred Hopkin, who used to make the 'bullets' for Chambers to fire.

There was a fellow called Parkinson, too – Jack Parkinson – whom goalkeepers learned to fear. He was a local lad who made his name with Liverpool just before the First World War, especially when he scored 30 goals in 31 games (the team altogether scored 78) in season 1909-10, when Liverpool finished second in the table. In 181 games between 1904 and 1914, Parkinson scored 116 goals, and he became an England International, like so many later Liverpool players. Jack Parkinson shared with Roger Hunt the distinction of topping the list of League marksmen in a season.

Mention of Roger Hunt brings us closer to the present, when the supporters who flock to Anfield hail the current heroes such as Kevin Keegan, yet many are not too old to recall names of the past like Balmer, Hodgson, Stubbins, Dave Hickson, Tony Hateley and company. Jackie Balmer began his career as an amateur – with Everton. He moved 'across the park' to Liverpool, and between 1935 and 1952 played almost 290 League games for the Anfield club, excluding wartime appearances. Altogether, he rattled in 97 League goals – including 10 in succession in three games during season 1946-7, when Liverpool won the Championship. The name of Balmer is familiar with football fans on Merseyside, but a stranger from South Africa became an idol of the Liverpool supporters, forty years and more ago. His name was Gordon Hodgson.

In 1924 he was on tour with a South African team, but he remained in this country to try his luck with Liverpool. He stayed to become Liverpool's No. 1 marksman, right through to the days of Roger Hunt. Hodgson scored 233 goals in 358 League games – and in season 1930-1, when he collected three England Caps, he scored 36 for his club. His career at Anfield lasted from 1925 to 1936, then he moved to Aston Villa and Leeds before hanging up his boots in 1939. When it came to goals, Hodgson, Hunt and Billy Liddell were the three most prolific scorers of them all for Liverpool, each of these men topping the 200 mark in League matches. But sandwiched between Hodgson and Hunt is the name of another famed marksman, Albert Stubbins, who was signed from Newcastle and quickly won the hearts of the Anfield faithful, while breaking the hearts of opposing defenders. Stubbins arrived with a scoring reputation – and he certainly lived up to it.

Nowadays, Albert is a journalist back in his native North-east; but, like so many who made their way to Anfield as professional footballers, he retains a warm affection for Liverpool and for the people who cheered him on match days. He recalls how the transfer came about; it turned out to be Liverpool on the toss of a coin, for Everton, too, wanted to sign him.

The representatives of both clubs were up at St James's Park, and Stubbins was being sought high and low that day. They flashed messages on the screen at the local cinemas, asking him to report to the Newcastle ground. When he arrived he learned that both the Merseyside clubs wanted to talk to him – so a coin was flipped to decide whom he should see first. It was Liverpool; and he signed for them, at a fee of £13 000, at that time one of the highest ever paid. The date was September, 1946.

Albert Stubbins who was signed from Newcastle at a fee of £13,000 in 1946 and proved one of Anfield's most prolific goal scorers.

Twenty-four goals came from Stubbins in his first season with Liverpool, and helped to win him a Championship medal. The following season, he scored 26 goals, and he finished with a record of 77 League goals in 159 games. Only Hunt, Liddell, St John and Jimmy Melia, of Liverpool's post-war marksmen, beat that tally, and they played many more games. The coin that came down 'heads' for Liverpool certainly spun luckily for the Anfield club.

Stubbins had scored 265 goals in 199 games for Newcastle, and he made his debut for his new team at Bolton. Liverpool won 3-1, and he scored the second goal. In his six seasons at Anfield he was destined to find the net many more times, and the older ones among the Liverpool fans still talk about 'the goal in the snow.' It was the sixth round of the FA Cup against Birmingham at Anfield, and the score was 1-1 when Liddell fired a free-kick hard from the left, and only a couple of feet or so above the ground, which was covered in snow and ice. Stubbins raced for the ball, flung himself full length – and the ball went in off his head like a rocket. Liverpool finished up the victors by 4-1, and Stubbins claimed three of the goals.

Stubbins also recalls two other games which gave him tremendous satisfaction – as well as goals – for totally different reasons. One was against Wolves at Molineux, towards the end of season 1946-7. Wolves needed only a

Stubbins scoring one of his most brilliant goals, a header, during the match with Birmingham in March 1947. The fans still recall that – 'goal in the snow'.

The hand of friendship for opponent Puskas who commanded respect throughout football . . . here is Billy Liddell, who twice played for Great Britain against the Rest of Europe.

draw to win the League; Liverpool had to beat them to pip them for the title.

Even then, the following Saturday, Stoke would be Champions, should they manage to win their game. But Stoke lost, and Liverpool won their vital match at Molineux. It was a Stubbins goal which proved decisive, out of the three which were scored. South-African winger Bob Priday was in Liverpool's team, and he was only a youngster; just before the game Stubbins had a quiet word with him. Stubbins was up against one of the masters, centre-half Stan Cullis, and he warned Priday: 'If you pick the ball up fairly deep, near the half-way line, look up, and hit the ball past Cullis and between the full-backs. I'll do the rest.'

Priday duly found himself in possession, and as soon as Stubbins saw this he turned and raced forward, past Cullis and between the backs. As Cullis and Billy Wright chased him, and the backs converged to snuff out the danger, Stubbins got to the ball first, and as goalkeeper Bert Williams came out, the centre-forward pushed the ball past him and into the net. That goal remains one of the most precious Stubbins ever scored. It won the game for Liverpool – and the title.

Albert's other outstanding memory is of a game against Huddersfield, who were in danger of relegation. Just before the match, which was at Anfield, a telegram arrived for Stubbins. When he opened it, his brow furrowed, for it warned him that if he tried to get near enough to score he would get his leg broken. Stubbins did not say a word to anyone; but he was determined to ignore the threat. It had made him an angry man. Liverpool won, hammering Town 4-0 – and Stubbins scored all four goals.

Despite his North-east upbringing, and his affection for his native heath, Albert Stubbins is another who remembers Merseyside and Liverpool with great warmth. When Liverpool went to Wembley in the spring of 1974, Albert was torn with divided loyalties, for Newcastle were Liverpool's opponents. At first, he predicted a Newcastle victory, but when he learned that Newcastle had made a full-back switch because of injury, he changed his mind and forecast that Liverpool would win. He was right, and he helped Liverpool celebrate at their after-match banquet. He was a guest, too, at Newcastle's function some days later.

If Stubbins was popular at Anfield, the man they called 'The Flying Scot', Billy Liddell, was idolised. He became a Liverpool player when he was but sixteen years old, and although he did not make his bow in the League side

Three of Liverpool's greatest ever players; left to right, Tommy Smith, Ian St. John and Ron Yeats, talk over old times at a testimonial dinner given for St. John.

until he was twenty-four, he went on to set a new club record of 532 appearances in League and Cup. Eight times he finished as leading scorer, in a career which brought him 228 goals, and apart from winning Scotland honours, he – with Stanley Matthews – played for the Great Britain side against the Rest of Europe in 1947 and 1955.

The strongly built Liddell never had a lot to say for himself. But his deeds on the field of play – where he was fearless, and packed a deadly shot, as well as being swift when he was moving for or with the ball – did the talking for him. Despite his Scottish qualifications, Billy Liddell's accent has the

Ian St. John seen with the new Liverpool team before his testimonial game in 1973.

Liverpool stalwart Alun Evans seen in 1970 during a match with Huddersfield.

8
ROGER HUNT
Liverpool and England
LIVERPOOL
W. Shankly
R. Paisley
ENGLAND
T. Lawrence
C. Lawler
G. Byrne
G. Milne
R. Yeats
W. Stevenson
I. Callaghan
R Hunt
I. St. John
T. Smith
P. Thompson
G. Strong
G. Banks
G. Cohen
R. Wilson
N. Stiles
J. Charlton
R. Moore
A. Ball
R. Charlton
M. Peters
G. Hurst
AJAX
Holland
INTER MILAN
Italy
JUVENTUS
Italy
NANTES
France
BORUSSIA
DORTMUND
West Germany
COLOGNE
West Germany
MALMO
Sweden
BILBAO
Spain
ANDERLECHT
Belgium
REYKJAVIK
WEST GERMANY
FRANCE
WALES
EAST GERMANY
NORTHERN IRELAND
PORTUGAL
COVENTRY
PORTSMOUTH
CHELSEA
WOLVES
PORT VALE
WALSALL
G. Byrne
G. Milne
T. Smith
R. Yeats
G. Strong
I. Callaghan
R. Hunt

overtones of Merseyside, and he still lives and works in the area. Like Albert Stubbins, he was a guest of Liverpool at their 1974 FA Cup-final banquet, as were so many other former stalwarts, such as Ron Yeats, Alun Evans, Peter Thompson, Ian St John and Roger Hunt.

St John set another club record when Liverpool paid Motherwell £35 000 for the privilege of signing him. Bill Shankly was moved to say that this player was not merely the best centre-forward in these islands – he was the ONLY one. He kicked off with a hat-trick in a Liverpool Senior Cup final against Everton, and he never looked back; for after his arrival in 1961 he went on to play more than 400 games and score more than 100 goals for Liverpool. More than that; he also carved himself a special spot in Liverpool's history, for his was the goal in 1965 that defeated Leeds United at Wembley and took the FA Cup to Anfield for the first time in the club's history. Like Liddell, and players who had gone before him, St John won Caps for Scotland. And like many other players of the post-war era, he acknowledges that playing for Liverpool was one of the great experiences of his life.

So we come to one of St John's team-mates of the 1960s, when Liverpool were all-conquering at home, if not abroad: Roger Hunt. He won a World Cup medal with England in 1966, and this willing workhorse exhausted himself in the cause of club and country. He set records as he went along, too – 245 goals in 401 League matches, 18 FA Cup goals, 17 European goals, 41 goals in Liverpool's promotion season of 1961-2, and 34 Caps for England.

The fans dubbed him 'Sir Roger' and 'Gentleman Roger', and not without cause. Fearless, like Liddell, he had the same sort of equable temperament which enabled him to shrug aside, for the most part, the harsh treatment defenders at times meted out to him. It says much for the hold that Billy Liddell had on the Liverpool supporters that a benefit match in 1960 brought a crowd of 38 789 and receipts of £6000; but even this was dwarfed by the turn-out for Roger Hunt's testimonial game, for despite a downpour, 56 000 people flocked to Anfield to honour him on his official farewell appearance.

When Hunt and St John had departed, people on Merseyside – and further afield – speculated how Liverpool could possibly replace such giants. But Liverpool rebuilt their team, brought new faces into the side, and carried on almost as if nothing had happened. In the 1960s they won the League, the FA Cup and the League again, in successive years (1964-5-6); and the new team did not take long to find its feet. In 1971, Liverpool went back to Wembley,

Liverpool and England star Roger Hunt with a plaque presented to him as a record of his ten years at Anfield.

Left to right, defender Phil Thompson, Liverpool Captain Emlyn Hughes and Alec Lindsay.

only to lose to Arsenal; but two years later, they won not only the Championship, but the UEFA Cup – the first English club to achieve this double. In 1974 they again made the trek to Wembley, this time to whip Newcastle decisively. By then, the new heroes had arrived: Kevin Keegan, who scored twice against Newcastle; John Toshack, Steve Heighway, Alex Lindsay, Brian Hall, Peter Cormack, Phil Thompson and so on. Plus, of course, Ian Callaghan and Tommy Smith, with Chris Lawler as the substitute. In the later stages of season 1975-6, as Liverpool sought yet again

Roger Hunt acknowledges the applause of the Kop after scoring at Anfield in April 1972.

to complete a League-UEFA Cup double, a new scoring sensation burst upon the Anfield scene. He was a flame-haired, nineteen-year-old named David Fairclough, and his ability to beat opponents and rifle home goals with either foot electrified the fans, and had shrewd judges predicting that he would shoot to stardom. Even his manager, Bob Paisley, acknowledged that the lad was something special. Like Byrne, Smith, Lawler and Callaghan, Fairclough was another of the famous Liverpool Lads.

All the players mentioned have contributed towards the making of another chapter in Liverpool's story. For while this is the story of a club, it is essentially one about people, the folk who shape the destinies of a football club, and give it life, warmth and hope for the future.

4 Ten men at the helm

In a sport where some clubs have constantly hired and fired managers with startling rapidity, Liverpool have achieved a reputation for keeping their managers, for since 1893, when the club first came into League football, they have had only ten team bosses, including the man now at the helm, Bob Paisley. Some clubs have had this number of managers in little more than ten years, for this is the hot seat of football, and generally acknowledged as a hazardous occupation.

Liverpool's first two managers, in the dim and distant past, also acted as secretary of the club. There was W.E. Barclay, and he was followed by Tom Watson, who stayed at Anfield from 1896 until 1920 when he died. The next manager, David Ashworth, stayed only a short time because he joined Oldham Athletic after two years at Anfield, and after him came the first of several former players who have graduated to the managerial chair. He was Matt McQueen, and he had also had the distinction of being a director of the club. He held the job until 1928 – after losing a leg in an accident, he resigned – and following him was George Patterson, who had already held the post of secretary for some years. When George Kay arrived from Southampton, to take over as manager in 1936, Patterson reverted to his original role.

George Kay was fifteen years at Anfield, and it was he who signed Albert Stubbins from Newcastle, on that decisive day which saw Liverpool beat Everton by the flip of a coin.

Kay was a man who commanded respect in football, for he had been a West Ham player of some note and he captained that team against Bolton in the FA Cup final of season 1922-3. This was the first Cup Final to be held at Wembley, and the final which became famous because of the crowd scenes and the 'White Horse' drama. Kay was a man of forceful character, and he held away until ill-health brought about his retirement in 1951. One of the players who came under his influence at Anfield was Cliff Lloyd, who spent several seasons with Liverpool and went on to become the secretary of the Professional Footballers' Association.

Kay was a Mancunian, and he was succeeded by another man from that city, Don Welsh, who had been a player – guesting for Liverpool during the war years – and then secretary-manager at Brighton. Welsh had earned himself a reputation by scoring six goals against Southport in December, 1944, in a game which Liverpool won 12-1, and he was later invited to join the Anfield coaching staff, but could not obtain his release from his club, Charlton Athletic. When George Kay resigned, Liverpool offered the job to Welsh, and he stayed five years as the manager of Anfield.

The departure of Welsh brought Phil Taylor, another name familiar to Liverpool supporters into the managerial fold at Anfield, for he had been a wing-half with the club. By the time he became manager, Liverpool had slipped into the Second Division. Taylor had signed for Liverpool from Bristol Rovers in 1936, and he skippered the team in the 1950 FA Cup final. He became chief coach at Anfield, then manager, and he stayed to complete twenty-one years' service with the club in one capacity or another. When he resigned in November, 1959, he went into business in Liverpool. The club was still in the Second Division, but the dawn of a new and significant era was not far away.

The late Mr T.V. Williams, who became Liverpool president, was the chairman of the club when Bill Shankly was offered the job as manager. He met Shankly to discuss the job, and, as a result, Liverpool acquired a manager who fitted into the scheme of things, yet retained complete independence. However, the first game under Shankly's charge did not herald the transformation that was to take place. Liverpool lost at home to Cardiff, who scored four goals at Anfield. Liverpool were to lose very few on their own ground after that, however!

Then, as now, Bob Paisley was at Anfield, and he remembers how Shankly used to come into the dressing-room to borrow a ball and a track suit, and disappear to Huddersfield on Sunday mornings. The backroom staff at Anfield eventually learned that Shankly was playing football with the locals on the other side of the Pennines – it had become a ritual during his days as the manager of Huddersfield Town. From the start, Shankly devoted his attention to the job of getting Liverpool out of the Second Division, and although there were one or two near-misses, success came before long.

At the end of season 1959-60, Liverpool finished in third place in the table, with 50 points; and the next season followed the same pattern – third again, this time with 52 points. Season 1961-2 saw Liverpool third-time lucky, for they finished top of the table with 62 points. They had won twenty-seven

The date is 1951, and the occasion is the arrival of new Liverpool manager Don Welsh. Left to right in this picture are J.C. Rouse (Club Secretary), Jack Balmer, Don Welsh, Phil Taylor (Liverpool Captain), George Richards (Liverpool Chairman).

Don Welsh and the Liverpool team.

games, lost only seven, and scored 99 goals while conceding a miserly 43. The days of glory were about to begin. Since then, Liverpool have never finished lower than eighth in the First Division table, and Shankly's achievements as their manager have become legendary.

The man had a burning enthusiasm for the game, and he was able to charge everyone else with this spirit. Under him, Liverpool became recognised as a team which never surrendered, which would go on fighting

In 1956 former Liverpool Captain Phil Taylor became Manager at Anfield.

even a seemingly lost cause until the final whistle had gone and the result was beyond doubt, one way or the other. Sometimes he would come out with what appeared to be outrageous statements, to emphasise his points. Even when Liverpool had lost, he appeared to be able to find cogent arguments in their favour, and you went away wondering if they had really won, and you had merely dreamed the actual result of the game.

Stories about Shankly circulated in abundance; and they only served to make the man seem larger than life. There was the one about a team winning at Anfield – an unexpected victory it was, indeed – and some wag in the Press box, imitating Shankly's gravel-like voice, rasped: 'The Fitba' League wull nivver accept this result!'

There was the occasion when someone, it was said, had talked to Shankly about football being a matter of life and death, so far as he was concerned, and he was reputed to have replied, his face deadly serious! 'Life and death? It's MORE serious than that ...'

There was the journalist who wrote about Liverpool's achievements in the 1960s, when they won the League, the FA Cup and the League again in successive seasons. Shankly read the article, and complimented the man who had written it. Then he added: 'But you missed one thing out – we won the FA Charity Shield, as well!' And there was not the ghost of a smile on Shankly's face as he uttered this gentle rebuke.

Even now, after he has retired, it is difficult to find one single reason for Shankly's incredible success at Liverpool. Players past and present have tried to sum it up; they all put forward their versions of the way Shankly operated, the words he would speak before they went out to play, and the staccato style of the man. They respected him, and believed in what he told them, about themselves and about their opponents. Perhaps the truth is that here was a man whose attitude was always indomitable, and whose intensity of feeling for the game and for his team inspired the people he was moulding.

Shankly was a manager who could sharply criticise and yet also a man who could show real compassion. Often, he would decline to comment about other teams, but he was always concerned to make his own men feel superior to the opposition in every way. Bob Paisley remembers how, when the tactical board was out, Shankly would literally put players such as George Best and Bobby Charlton in his pocket. He would sweep away the counters representing such stars, and concentrate on what HIS team was going to do to the opposition.

One member of the staff at Anfield, Ken Addison, secretary-treasurer of the Development Association, recalls seeing Bill Shankly come out of the players' room at the end of a briefing for a game against Leeds United. Bill was smiling to himself, and Ken was allowed to share the joke. Bill had had the board out, and he chuckled as he said to Ken Addison: 'We won, Kenny, we won ... 3-1. And that Bremner – he never got a kick!' Twentyfour hours later, when the actual game was played, Liverpool did win, by the only goal of the game.

One of the greatest Managers of all time, Bill Shankly.

Bill Shankly, after Liverpool's victory in the FA Cup at Wembley in 1974.

Whether at home or abroad, Shankly was a character well worth observing. He would look you straight in the eye when he was talking, as if defying you to contradict him; very few people did. The bald facts of Liverpool's success speak for themselves – and for Shankly's achievements as their manager. In their first season after their return to Division 1, they finished eighth, and followed this in successive years by finishing first, seventh, first, fifth, third, second, fifth, fifth, third, first and second. They won the FA Cup in 1965 for the first time in the club's history; they went to Wembley again in 1971, only to lose, and in 1974, this time to win. They rached the semi-finals of the European Cup, the final of the Cup-winners' Cup, they won the UEFA Cup, and they were competing in Europe for the eleventh successive season when Shankly finally laid aside the managerial burden. Oh, yes – and they won the FA Charity Shield.

Bill Shankly with the Bell's Scotch Whisky Football Manager of the Year Cup.

Shankly spent big money on signing players, and he delved into the lower divisions to clinch bargain buys like Kevin Keegan and Ray Clemence. He finished his career after having moulded one great side, by producing another all-conquering team, and it was typical of the man that he signed off with a flourish by securing the transfer of Ray Kennedy from Arsenal for £200 000. When he retired as manager, Liverpool could field a team of full Internationals, and on the day he made his official farewell appearance, walking round the ground on a lap of honour, he was greeted by rapturous applause which was clearly tinged with sadness. 'It was,' he said, 'an awesome occasion.' And his face was suitably solemn. As he scanned the luxurious lounge where he stood sipping a cup of tea, he added: 'It's been a proud day, yet a sad one. Sad, because of what it means; but proud, because I can think that I played some part in building all this.'

When Shankly shook the Soccer world by revealing his intention to retire, there was immediate speculation as to who would – who COULD – follow him. One or two names were canvassed by outsiders, but it really was inevitable that Liverpool would keep the job 'in the family.' No one was surprised when they handed the job of team manager to Bob Paisley. Here was a man who had been at Shankly's shoulder throughout all the campaigns; here was a man who also embodied the spirit of Liverpool. His first reaction: 'It's a challenge ... but I'm not daunted by it.'

Bob Paisley is a likeable, smiling – but shrewd – Geordie who has made Merseyside his home for many years now. He had been at Liverpool long

ADM IRAL
ADM IRAL

before Bill Shankly became manager. He was 'part of the furniture' at Anfield, and the players knew and respected him. Bob joined Liverpool as a player in 1939, soon after helping Bishop Auckland to carry off the FA Amateur Cup, and he made 252 appearances in League games, between 1946 and 1954. He was a terrier-like wing-half, and he applied himself to the job with immense enthusiasm.

There was a day – many years ago – when he considered asking Liverpool for a transfer. It was when Liverpool went to Wembley and Paisley was not in the team, after having played in previous rounds of the Cup. But Paisley kept his own counsel in the end and stayed on. That omission from the Cup-final side was, he still admits, a tremendous disappointment to him; but he also acknowledges that when he went to Wembley with Liverpool in 1965, as their trainer, he felt compensated for not having played there for the team. Player, trainer, coach, assistant to the manager, and finally team manager; so Bob Paisley has risen through the ranks at Anfield. It was typical of him, when Shankly announced that he was retiring, that Paisley should say he was prepared to serve the club in any capacity. Paisley had figured in Liverpool's Championship side of the season 1946-7, and he knew what was demanded of players – and of managers. 'We've been in the boiling pot all the time,' he said, with reference to Liverpool's achievements during the Shankly era. 'We haven't been competing for twopence-halfpenny trophies.' So he well knew what he was being asked to do, in following Shankly; and he did not shrink from the challenge.

Somewhere in Bob Paisley's make-up there is a streak of tempered steel. He is what they call in Geordie-land a canny fellow, easy to talk to, ready to smile, but his own man, just like the fellow he succeeded. Seldom, if ever, can a manager have had such a rapport with the fans as Shankly had with the Liverpool Kop; and Paisley, wisely, was quick to recognise this. As he said: I hope I can let the team do the talking for me.' Certainly the team did its best, in season 1974-5, as the weeks passed. Liverpool were still Liverpool – the ones all the others had to beat.

Paisley's style is not quite the same as Shankly's, but it is nonetheless effective. In naming this former player as team manager to succeed Shankly, Liverpool had acted wisely and, as their chairman, John W. Smith, said, preserved continuity and stability. The ranks had been closed so that it did not even appear that there had been a gap.

Wembley, August 1974, and Bill Shankly leads out the Liverpool team for the last time for the match with Leeds for the FA Charity Shield. Brian Clough heads the Leeds line up.

Managers past and present, Bob Paisley on the left and Bill Shankly on the right.

At the end of Bob Paisley's first season in management, Liverpool finished second in the League. It was an achievement with which Paisley could be well satisfied – but he knew that supporters would expect consistent success. The following season, 1975-6, Paisley and his team scored success after success. With half a dozen teams fiercely contesting the Championship in the First Division, the outcome remained undecided until the very end of the season. Leeds, Derby and Manchester United all stumbled in their pursuit of Championship honours, losing matches that the experts anticipated they would win; but Queens Park Rangers finished with a victory flourish, so that Liverpool had to win or draw their last match of the season at Wolverhampton Wanderers if the Championship was to be theirs. They won.

In addition, Paisley steered Liverpool through to victory in the UEFA Cup. The fans who had once chanted Shankly's name with such avid dedication now hailed Paisley as the new master of Anfield. As Paisley commented, 'It's been nice to have been acknowledged a little bit.' Certainly Bob Paisley had shown that he could measure up to the most demanding task in football – keeping Liverpool to the fore – and well merited the award of Manager of the Year.

What the future holds, in terms of honours, is difficult – impossible – to predict. However there seems no reason to doubt that Liverpool will be among the pacesetters for the next few years, and that neither club nor manager will lose that foresight which has kept the club at the top of the tree for more than a decade.

Bob Paisley pictured with his wife and three children.

Bob Paisley and the Liverpool first team squad at the start of the 1974-5 season. Fifteen players . . . and on the back row (left to right) it's Phil Thompson, Chris Lawler, Ray Kennedy, Frank Lane, Ray Clemence, John Toshack, Phil Boersma, Peter Cormack, Steve Heighway. Front row: Brian Hall, Ian Callaghan, Tommy Smith, team-manager Bob Paisley, Emlyn Hughes, Alec Lindsay, Kevin Keegan.

5 Champions? You can say that nine times over!

No club had won the Championship of the First Division more times than Liverpool, and only one club – Arsenal – had equalled Liverpool's record of eight Championship Successes. Then in 1975-6, Liverpool captured the First Division title for the ninth time, a unique feat. Liverpool have also finished as Champions of the Second Division no fewer than four times; and on three of these occasions they won promotion at the first time of asking.

Liverpool's first excursion into the honours race was as long ago as season 1893-4 – their first in League football – when they gained 50 points out of a possible 56, and thereby lifted the Championship of Division 2. It was a striking success, indeed, for Liverpool won every single one of their 14 home games (shades of things to come!) and won the test match which decided promotion. Their opponents in that game were Newton Heath, later to become known as Manchester United, a club who followed hard on Liverpool's heels in that they have taken the First Division title seven times themselves.

Liverpool were undefeated when they gained promotion to the First Division, but their joy was short-lived, for in 1895 they were relegated, but regained their First Division status the following year when they ›ok 46 points out of 60, and five points from the four test matches they had to play. Having finished top of Division 2, sixteenth in Division 1, and top of Division 2 again, Liverpool then began the business of consolidating their First Division status, and they finished a highly respectable fifth, in season 1896-7, with 33 points from 30 games.

The next season, with 28 points, they had slipped to ninth place, but the season after that, they collected 43 points from 34 matches, to finish in second place. Season 1899-1900 was one of disappointment, for Liverpool could do no better than finish in tenth place, with 33 points; then came their first success in the Championship stakes. In season 1900-1, Liverpool won 19 of their 34 games, drew 7 and lost 8, to finish top of the pack with 45 points. The heady success of that season, however, was shortly to be followed by a hangover, because in consequent seasons Liverpool then dropped to eleventh, fifth and seventeenth, which meant that they were relegated again to the Second Division.

Jackie Balmer, Captain of the Liverpool team which won the First Division Championship in 1947.

Once more a transformation took place, for Liverpool did what was becoming a habit for them – they finished top of the Second Division, with 58 points, and went on to achieve a double Championship success by heading the First Division, with 51 points. That was the start of an unbroken run of First Division football which took Liverpool from season 1905-6 up to the First World War, continued when football was resumed in season 1919-20, carried on until the outbreak of the Second World War, and was maintained right through until season 1953-4. In those 39 seasons of uninterrupted First Division football, Liverpool won the Championship four times – seasons 1905-6, 1921-2, 1922-3, and 1946-7. They collected 57 points when they won in season 1921-2, by which time the programme entailed 42 League games, and excelled themselves the following term, when they picked up 60 points by winning 26 matches and losing only 8.

Once, in season 1909-10, they also finished in second place; and between the two world wars they made a bold showing when they were not taking the title by finishing in fourth place three times, and fifth once. When they celebrated the return of peacetime football by winning the Championship in season 1946-7, they collected 57 points from their 42 games, winning 25 and drawing seven. Oddly enough, there was one season when they might have expected to win the title and could do no better than finish in seventh place, for in season 1934-5 they scored 85 goals, compared with 63, 70 and 84 in their three Championship seasons which involved 42 League games. However, the season in which they finished seventh told its own story – Liverpool lost 16 games, and conceded 88 goals.

Liverpool, indeed, had several experiences of scoring close on a century of goals, and yet finishing well below the top place in the table. When they finished fourth, on three occasions, they did so with a relative economy of goals, scoring 59, 63 and 63, and conceding 44, 35 and 55. Yet three times they hit more than 80 goals, but had no trophies to show for their efforts. In season 1927-8 they scored 84 goals, but conceded 87, to finish sixteenth; in season 1930-1, they scored 86 goals to 85, and finished ninth; and in season 1931-2 they scored 81 goals and conceded 93, to finish tenth. In the spell between the wars, their highest scoring tally was 90 goals, in season 1928-9; they conceded 64 goals, collected 46 points, and were fifth in the table.

The Championship season of 1946-7, immediately after the Second World War, did not see more successes – rather, the pendulum began to swing the other way, as Liverpool went on to finish eleventh, twelfth, eighth, ninth, eleventh, seventeenth, and then twenty-second – which resulted in a drop into the Second Division once more. This time, instead of climbing straight back, they did no more than finish an inauspicious eleventh, despite having scored 92 goals. For they conceded 96, and with 16 defeats as well as 16 victories, collected only a point a game. Then came the upsurge which was to carry Liverpool into the First Division, and invest them with an aura of greatness. In quick succession, Liverpool finished third, third, fourth, fourth again, third twice more. It was a time of frustration for the club and its faithful supporters, as near-miss followed near-miss, and one began to wonder if there was a jinx on Liverpool as they strove to break the bonds of Second Division serfdom. Regularly, they amassed 50 points or more per season; and regularly, they saw other clubs finish just ahead of them.

Bill Shankly had arrived, and everyone hoped Liverpool's luck would change under this dynamic manager: it did, too, as Shankly, who was installed as manager in December, 1959, saw his side succeed at the third attempt. They finished third, third again, and then as Second Division champions, with 62 points, in season 1961-2. Liverpool had won 27 games and lost only 7; they had scored 99 goals and conceded 43. The balance, at last, was right.

Liverpool's re-entry into the First Division was not marked by an immediate salvo which proclaimed them as the top team in the land, for they finished merely in a respectable eighth place, with 44 points. Twice in the following three years, however, they were to bring the League Championship trophy to Anfield, as Shankly cemented together what came to be regarded as a truly great team. Liverpool won the title in season 1963-4, and the following season had to be satisfied with seventh place and the FA Cup for consolation. Then they took the title again in 1965-6, and were in contention for the honours season by season, after that.

During Shankly's reign Liverpool never fell below eighth place in the First Division. They finished fifth, after their second title success during the 1960s, then they were third, then they were runners-up, and then fifth again. By this time the great side of the 1960s was in the process of being broken up. Shankly himself admitted that he had thought this team would go on longer than it did; but when he decided that changes needed to be made, he was not swayed by sentiment, although it grieved him to demote players who had done so much for the club. Gradually, a new-look Liverpool side took shape. In one way, the transition was so swift that it seemed there had never been a hiatus, yet, it was spread over several seasons, as established players fought to retain their places.

In the end, it appeared to have been a swift and smooth transition because Liverpool never lost their impetus, their appetite for the fray – and, above all, their ability to beat the best in the bid for honours. Tommy Smith, one of the seasoned campaigners – he was a youngster in Liverpool's 1965 FA Cup-winning side – admitted that he thought the 'new' team would need a couple of years to settle, before the honours were in sight again. Instead, Liverpool swept to Wembley in 1971, and although they lost to Arsenal, they had made their presence felt in no uncertain manner. May, 1971, saw Liverpool finish fifth behind Arsenal, Leeds, Spurs and Wolves; May, 1972, saw them finish third behind Derby County and Leeds – and it had been a white-hot finale to the Championship battle, for the issue was decided only at the very end. Derby had to wait to see if either Liverpool or Leeds could beat their 58-point total; they learned they were Champions while on holiday in Majorca!

Liverpool had, indeed, given warning of what was to come – but even they did not realise then that season 1972-3 would see them go through sixty-six competitive matches to capture not only the First Division title, but the UEFA Cup. On Saturday, 12 August, 1972, Liverpool began with a 2-0 victory over Manchester City at Anfield. When the first League tables were published, and three games had been played, Arsenal were in the lead with six points, and Liverpool were second with five. After five matches, Liverpool hit the top, with nine points out of ten; then, with two more games played, they surrendered the leadership to Arsenal again, and, in fact, they had slipped to sixth in the table. Was that first surge of power merely a flash in the pan? Had Liverpool flattered, only to deceive?

The answer from Anfield came, loud and clear. Everton went to the top, while Liverpool edged into fourth place – next it was Everton, Ipswich, Leeds, Arsenal, Liverpool. THEN it was Liverpool in the lead, with ten games gone, and as the old year faded, no one had been able to overhaul them. Liverpool were still lording it over the rest, after twenty-five matches. Not until thirty games had been played did Liverpool slip from the top of the table – and then it was for only a few brief days, as Arsenal made their bid for a takeover. Liverpool, however, were not to be denied; after thirty-one matches they had

Ace Liverpool scorer, Kevin Keegan.

Republic of Ireland International and Liverpool player Steve Heighway.

taken over the leadership once more, and they remained ahead of everyone, right through to the last game of the season.

By Easter Monday the challenge had been narrowed down to Leeds and Arsenal. Liverpool met Leeds at Anfield. It was a full house, and the atmosphere was electric. At the end of the ninety minutes, there was little doubt about the destination of the First Division Championship, Liverpool had vanquished Leeds, Arsenal had slipped, and it needed a mathematical miracle to prevent Shankly's team taking the title. In fact, so long as Liverpool drew their final game against Leicester, at Anfield, even a mathematical miracle could not change things. Liverpool duly drew, 0-0, to put the whole issue beyond doubt.

Their season still had not finished, for there was the UEFA Cup final against Borussia Mönchengladbach. And again, Liverpool were not to be denied, although they were given a scare. It was a season of success, and the silverware Liverpool collected told the story.

Liverpool had won the League Championship and the UEFA Cup; their reserves had won the Central League title and the Lancashire County Cup; the 'B' team had won the Supplementary Cup, and were top of their division in the Lancashire League. Ian Callaghan had broken Billy Liddell's record of 532 appearances for the club; Chris Lawler had become only the third player to play 500 games for Liverpool; total League gates at Anfield set a new record of 1 010 150 (average 48 102); Liverpool's eight First Division title successes, plus their four Second Division Championships, gave them a total of twelve titles – more than any other club in England.

Liverpool did not quite make it, when it came to breaking yet another record, for they needed 6 goals from their two EUFA ties to beat the tally of 110 set in season 1895-6; in the end, they had to settle for a total of 108 goals – but who was really worried? Liverpool, who had a run of 18 games unbeaten during the season, did break the club record by winning 37 of the 66 matches they played – the previous best was 31, in season 1965-6 – and they equalled the record for the number of competitive games played in one season by an English club. Leeds had set the record, with 66 games in season 1967-8, and Tottenham had matched this in season 1971-2, when they had won the UEFA Cup which now passed to Liverpool.

It was a fitting reward for Liverpool's prodigious efforts through a season which had proved so very, very long. And while they could not quite match it the following season, they proved to be the only team who were ever really in with a chance of catching the eventual champions, Leeds United. Liverpool had to settle for second place, which they had occupied since 1 December, 1973, and it says a great deal for the Anfield men that they not only outstripped third-placed Derby County, who had 48 points, but achieved a tally of 57 points themselves which might well, in another season, have been good enough to clinch the Championship.

Liverpool had to settle for finishing second, also, in Bob Paisley's first season of management, although that was a fine start for the man who had had to follow Bill Shankly. Season 1975-6 began on an inauspicious note, for Liverpool lost their first game, away against Queen's Park Rangers; no one realised then that by the end of the season, Liverpool would have played 59 competitive matches, reached the final of the UEFA Cup once more, seen off the Championship challenge of teams like Manchester United, Derby County and Leeds – and be left in a situation which meant they needed a draw (up to 2-2 would do) or a win from their final game against Wolves at Molineux, to take the title from the team that had inflicted that defeat on the opening day of the season.

After three games, Liverpool lay thirteenth in the First Division table; an unaccustomed position, indeed, for them. After five games, they had climbed to eighth, after six they lay fifth; then they slipped to seventh, pulled back to fourth, retreated to eighth, and forced their way to fourth spot again. By then, a dozen matches had been and gone. Liverpool were on the fringe of the pacesetters for a few more weeks, then they emerged in second place to Derby, after they had completed 16 games. Up to then, the various leaders had been Manchester United, Queen's Park Rangers and West Ham. At the half-way stage, it was Rangers, Liverpool, United and Derby, in that order. The takeover bid had still to be made.

Liverpool edged into top place with a 2-0 home win over Rangers, in their twenty-second match of the season, and they kept their lead until Manchester United moved clear, after 25 games. It was United, Leeds and Liverpool – with the Anfield club having played one more match than their rivals. With 28 games gone, Liverpool led the way once more, level on 39 points with United, but superior in the matter of goal average. They and United also had a game in hand on third-placed Rangers, who were one point adrift. With 32 games played, Liverpool were still on top; but after 34 games, Rangers led the

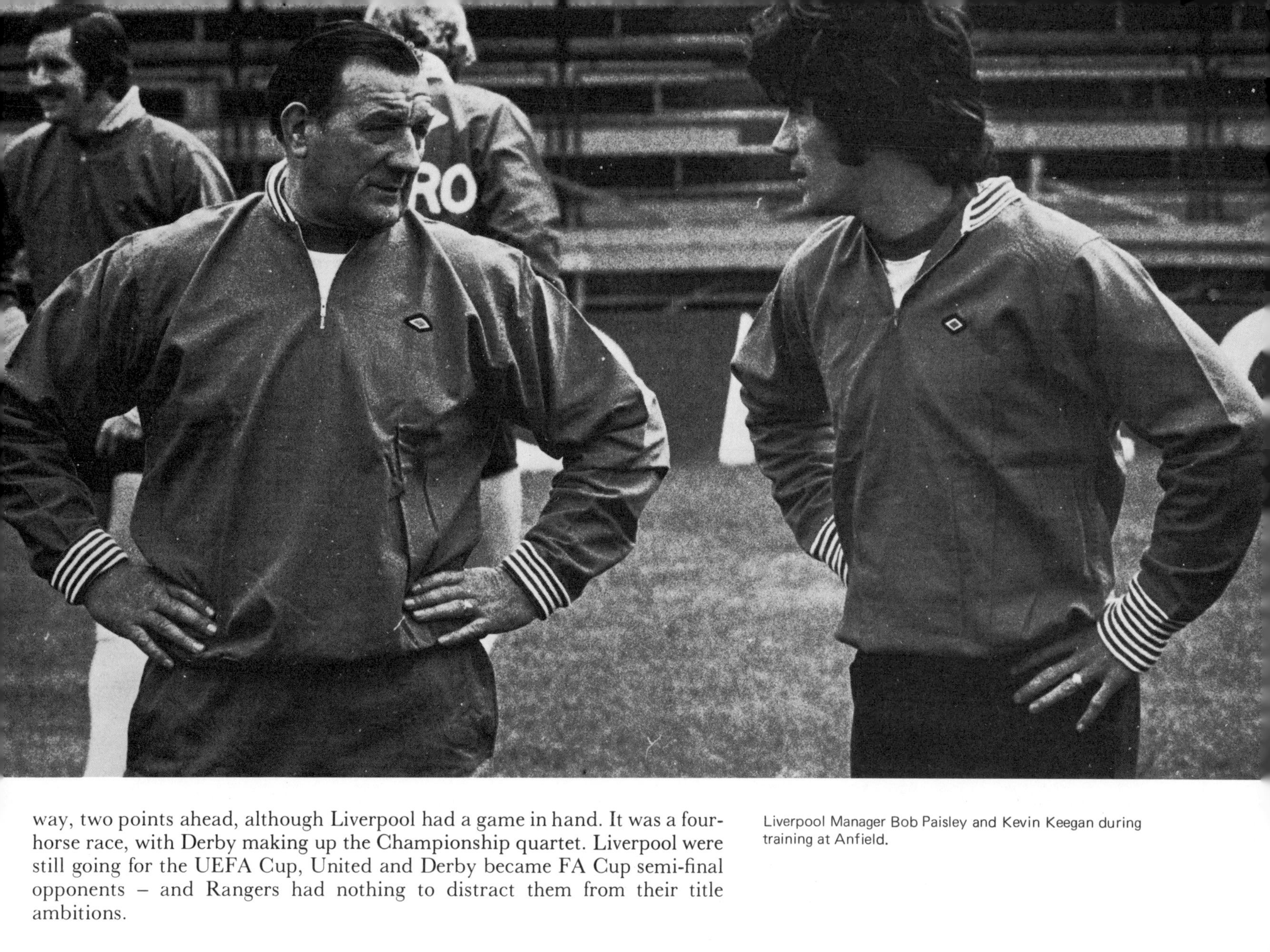

way, two points ahead, although Liverpool had a game in hand. It was a four-horse race, with Derby making up the Championship quartet. Liverpool were still going for the UEFA Cup, United and Derby became FA Cup semi-final opponents – and Rangers had nothing to distract them from their title ambitions.

Liverpool Manager Bob Paisley and Kevin Keegan during training at Anfield.

England and Liverpool goalkeeper, Ray Clemence.

United vanquished Derby in the Cup, and Dave Mackay's team began to fade from the Championship tussle. But Rangers were on a remarkable run, which saw them take 23 points out of 24, and the title rivals were fast running out of matches. Rangers won at Newcastle with a goal in the dying seconds, and they began to be the bookies' favourites for the Championship – yet Liverpool and United could still overhaul them, IF they won and won and won. The crunch came at Easter, when Liverpool hammered Stoke 5-3 at Anfield, and Norwich scored a 3-2 home win over Rangers, while United managed a 2-1 victory over Everton. Liverpool were back on top, with 56 points and two games to go. Rangers lay second, one point behind, and also with two games left. United, four points behind Liverpool, had two matches in hand on them, so they could still do it.

On Easter Monday morning, Rangers kicked off their home match against Arsenal; and 90 minutes later, Liverpool knew they would still have to win the title the hard way. Rangers had been victorious, and leap-frogged back into the leadership, having taken 27 points out of 30. Liverpool that afternoon faced a really tough assignment, against Manchester City, at Maine Road, while United were at Burnley. Liverpool, who had blooded nineteen-year-old David Fairclough in a match at Middlesbrough earlier in the season – the Anfield Reds then became the first team to score and to win at Ayresome during the season – threw him into the fray against Manchester City.

Even before the 5-3 win over Stoke, manager Bob Paisley had told Fairclough he would be playing for the full 90 minutes at Maine Road, and in view of his recent performances, when he had scored goals that won crucial games, everyone wondered what sort of impact he would make against Manchester City. He soon showed that he could beat men – he went past them at times as if they did not exist. But little more than 15 minutes from the end of the match, it was still stalemate, at 0-0. Then Fairclough made an explosive impact, racing through and setting up a chance which Steve Heighway tucked away; and in the closing minutes of the game, Fairclough himself sped past toiling City defenders twice in quick succession, and scored goals which gave Liverpool a 3-0 victory, and put them back on top of the table, with 58 points, one ahead of Queen's Park Rangers.

Manchester United had won at Burnley, and if they defeated Stoke the following Wednesday, they would edge closer to their two title rivals. Liverpool and Rangers sat back and waited – and Stoke went to Old Trafford, and WON. That meant United could not catch the leaders; and the onus was on Rangers to win their final game of the season, at home to Leeds, leaving Liverpool to face Wolves at Molineux on 4 May, and see if they could do any better. Rangers, in fact, beat Leeds 2-0, climbed back to the top of the table, and left Liverpool pondering their last three matches – all of them, as manager Bob Paisley said, Cup finals. There was the two-legged UEFA Cup final against FC Bruges and, sandwiched between those games, the vital, last League game at Molineux.

Goal average had been playing a part in everyone's calculations for a week or two, and the situation when Liverpool went to Molineux was crystal clear. One point would give Liverpool the Championship, provided they drew no score, 1-1 or 2-2; if they drew 3-3, then Rangers would be proclaimed champions. If Liverpool won, of course, they would finish a point ahead of their rivals. Although Liverpool conceded a goal early in the match, Toshack made it 2-1 in Merseyside's favour and Kennedy completed the rout by scoring a third Liverpool goal. So the League Championship went to Anfield for a record ninth time.

6 'We've all been to Wembley!'

When Liverpool went to Wembley in 1971 they had two of their keenest fans rooting for them – the surviving members of the FA Cup Final side which met Burnley in 1914 at Crystal Palace. That final was the first time Royalty had attended – King George V presented the cup – and the Liverpool side included Kenny Campbell and Bob Pursell. Campbell was the Liverpool goalkeeper in the 1914 final, and Pursell was at left-back. Burnley won the game, 1-0, and the goal was scored by a one-time Everton player, Bert Freeman, who played at centre-forward for Burnley that day. When the ball sped across from the wing, almost chest-high, Freeman caught it exactly right, and the ball fairly screamed into the net, hit a stanchion, and rocketed out again.

By 1971 Campbell was seventy-nine years old, and Pursell was eighty-two, but they both still retained a high regard for Liverpool, as do so many of the club's former players. Both men had been at Wembley in 1965, when Liverpool finally won the FA Cup by beating Leeds. Much had happened since then, but Liverpool were still going strong. And, of course, Liverpool have been to Wembley again, and won the Cup for a second time.

The first time Liverpool competed in the FA Cup tournament was in 1893, and it was in their second tie that they recorded their highest score in the competition – a 9-0 thrashing of Newton. It was the start of a long, and sometimes shaky road, as the Reds sought to capture one of the game's most glamorous trophies. Liverpool now have played more than 250 FA Cup-ties; they have been to the final of the competition five times, and finished as the victors twice.

Liverpool's first appearance in an FA Cup final, oddly enough, was also the last time the final was staged at Crystal Palace. Liverpool's team that day was: Campbell, Longworth, Pursell, Fairfoul, Ferguson, McKinlay, Sheldon, Metcalf, Miller, Lacey, Nicholl.

In 1950 Liverpool reached the final again, and this time they came up against Arsenal at Wembley. It was to be another disappointment for them, because two goals from Lewis ensured that the Cup went to the Gunners. The players who lined up for Liverpool in 1950 are, for the most part, mere faces in

Liverpool Captain Phil Taylor presents his team to King George VI before the start of the 1950 Cup Final at Wembley.

the crowd today, although one or two, such as Billy Liddell, get instant recognition when they visit Anfield.

In goal was Cyril Sidlow, and at right-back was Ray Lambert, a one-club man for twenty years. Ray's proud claim was that he became the youngest player ever signed by a First Division club. He was thirteen and a half when Liverpool spotted him playing for Flintshire and the Welsh Schoolboys. Lambert's full-back partner was Eddie Spicer, one of the players whose career had been interrupted by the war, for in 1939 he was a sixteen-year-old who had shown every sign of breaking through to top-class Soccer in the very near future. Spicer was one of the really unlucky players, because in 1951 his career was interrupted once more when he broke a leg. At the time he was being strongly tipped for England International honours. In 1953 a second fracture finally forced him to retire although he was still only thirty years old.

Liverpool's half-back line in 1950 read Taylor, Hughes and Jones. Phil Taylor was the skipper and he later became Liverpool's manager; he was an inspired and creative wing-half who became an England International. Unfortunately, he was destined not to walk up and collect the Cup that day at

Goal-keeper Cyril Sidlow clears a long centre during the 1950 Cup Final. Liverpool were beaten by Arsenal 2–0.

Liverpool Captain Phil Taylor shakes hands with Arsenal Captain Joe Mercer before the 1950 FA Cup Final.

Wembley, and that was a tremendous disappointment to him.

Centre-half Laurie Hughes was in England's 1950 World Cup squad, but a spate of injuries curtailed his appearances for club and country for a lengthy spell. Bill Jones, Liverpool's left-half at Wembley, had joined the club in 1938 and by the time Liverpool had reached the final in 1971, he was still serving the club as a scout. He did leave Anfield in 1954, to become player-manager with Ellesmere Port Town, but later swtiched his attention to spotting schoolboy talent on behalf of Liverpool.

Liverpool's outside-right was Jimmy Payne who admitted to having been an Everton fan – he was later signed by the Goodison club – and at inside-right was Kevin Baron, who had been a member of Liverpool's League Championship side two years previously. Baron was transferred to Southend in 1955, but a broken leg ended his playing career. Centre-forward Albert Stubbins is featured elsewhere in this book, and so is Billy Liddell; which leaves us with inside-left Willie Fagan, to complete the 1950 Cup-final team. Willie also played at half-back and on the wing for Liverpool, and he was club skipper in the Championship season of 1946-7. He had left Glasgow Celtic for Preston in 1936, and he was a team-mate of Bill Shankly. His appearance in the 1950 final was his second at Wembley, for he was in Preston's side which lost the Cup to Sunderland in 1937. Early the following season Fagan joined Liverpool, and Preston returned to Wembley to beat Huddersfield with that dramatic George Mutch penalty. So when Willie played in his second FA Cup final, he was again on the losing side, this time with Liverpool. Eventually, he left Anfield and went to Weymouth.

Fifteen years were to go by before Liverpool claimed a place in a Wembley final again, and this time it was third-time lucky, for they defeated Leeds 2-1 in extra time, through goals by Roger Hunt and Ian St John. By then Liverpool had emerged from a spell in the Second Division and were becoming prominent in the First – it was the start of the Shankly era which was to bring so many honours to the club. Liverpool's 1965 line-up was one that most Anfield fans will be able to recite without hesitation today: Lawrence, Lawler, Byrne; Strong, Yeats, Stevenson; Callaghan, Hunt, St John, Smith, Thompson. A team of strength and outstanding talent.

Many people reckoned that the final itself was not a memorable one; but it certainly contained plenty of drama, for Gerry Byrne, Liverpool's left-back, played for most of the game with a broken collar bone, and kept the secret of

Liverpool Centre-half and Skipper Ron Yeats holds up the FA Cup with Gordon Milne after Liverpool's victory over Leeds in the 1965 Final. Milne missed the match because of a knee injury.

his injury until Liverpool had won the Cup. Although Billy Bremner scored to give Leeds hope of snatching victory, it turned out to be Liverpool's day, with St John scoring the match-winning goal.

One man who shared in Liverpool's hour of glory, yet knew the disappointment of missing out as a participant in the game itself, was Gordon Milne, who had been signed by Bill Shankly from Preston, and a skilful wing-half who won England International honours. Milne had to drop out through injury, and that meant there was a place for Geoff Strong, who had been signed as a scoring forward from Arsenal but stayed at Anfield long enough to convince everyone that he could play well in virtually any position. At around £40 000, Strong turned out to be a bargain buy.

Strong was a Geordie; but two Scots also played a large part in Liverpool's success story of the 1960s. They were Willie Stevenson and Ron Yeats. Stevenson, who had been with Glasgow Rangers, went to try his luck in Australia, but returned to Britain to find that Liverpool wanted him. He, too, was a skilful half-back, a fine passer of the ball, and he possessed a shrewd Soccer brain.

Big Ron Yeats bestrode the centre of the defence like a giant. Bill Shankly once referred to him as 'The Colossus' – and the term stuck. Yeats was a genial giant of a player, a man who simply defied you to get past him. There were those who argued, especially during his later days at Anfield, that he could be beaten for speed without any question, but many opponents who thought they had beaten Yeats found to their chagrin that, somehow, they still had not got past him – or that, in trying, they had lost the ball. Yeats was signed from Dundee United in 1960, for £30 000 and, like Stevenson and St John, he turned out to be a true bargain. People used to talk of how Shankly had gone 'straight down the middle', when forging his first great Liverpool side — Lawrence in goal, Yeats barring the route to goal at centre-half, and St John up front to mastermind the attack and himself stick the ball past the opposing 'keeper. Yeats was indeed a dominating figure as he skippered Liverpool through hundreds of games, and he was regarded as unlucky not to win more Scottish Caps.

Mention has been made of Tommy Smith and Roger Hunt elsewhere, and so this leaves left-winger Peter Thompson, a pleasant character who had the gift of being able to dazzle opponents by his speed and brilliant ball control. Thompson was an entertainer who could torment the opposition and delight

Skipper Ron Yeats photographed with the FA Cup after the 1965 Final.

Liverpool Captain Emlyn Hughes with the FA Cup.

his own supporters. He, like Gordon Milne, was signed from Preston, where he had emerged as an outstanding centre-forward. At £40 000 he was another of Shankly's great investments. He became an England International, played more than 400 games for Liverpool, and finally, when it became clear that new faces were in the ascendancy at Anfield, he signed for Bolton, where, as an 'old hand', he contrived to make his influence felt as the Wanderers made a brave, but unsuccessful, bid to return to the First Division in season 1975-6.

Gradually, it became clear that Shankly was planning to change the look of his all-conquering side of the 1960s, and although it seemed hard to accept, one by one the established stars realised that they were increasingly on trial, and facing competition from the newcomers. Ray Clemence, signed from Scunthorpe, finally won the battle for the goalkeeping spot, and Larry Lloyd, signed from Bristol Rovers, replaced the giant Yeats at centre-half. Replacing a goal machine like Roger Hunt was probably one of the most difficult parts of the operation, and the same could be said about finding a successor to St John, while Thompson did not bow out without a fight to keep his place, either. But the new breed of footballers at Anfield was given its chance. Shankly, who had made the changes sadly, yet realistically, staked his reputation on the newcomers.

Suddenly, it seemed, they had begun to knit into a formidable combination – although, in the early days, there were many who compared the two teams, and claimed that the side of the 1960s was the greater. Even when Liverpool went to Wembley in 1971, to tackle Arsenal, some people were unconvinced about the quality of the side. It is true that, to some extent, they were still feeling their way. They realised that they were still in the shadow of the old team. But for better or worse, this was the Liverpool line-up for the 1971 Cup final: Clemence, Lawler, Lindsay, Smith, Lloyd, Hughes, Callaghan, Evans, Heighway, Toshack, Hall, Peter Thompson was the substitute who replaced Alun Evans for the last fifteen minutes of normal time. In the final analysis, Arsenal won, with goals from Graham and George, countering the goal struck by Steve Heighway.

The story of Ray Clemence has already been given in some detail elsewhere, and Lawler, Smith and Callaghan were survivors from the 1965 Cup-final team. One new name which was starting to make an impact was Alec Lindsay, signed from Bury for £65 000 in March, 1969. He was a former England Youth International who had begun to make his name as a half-back or forward who packed a lethal shot in his left foot. Some people claimed that he would turn out to be similar to Colin Bell, sold by Bury to Manchester City, but in his early days at Anfield Alec never seemed to be able to establish himself as a regular first-teamer, and there were times when his transfer seemed probable. Eventually, however, he was given the chance to settle in at left-back, and it was a role he took with confidence.

Since the days of Gerry Byrne, Liverpool had been looking around for a successor who could hold down the position of left-back, and in Lindsay they found their man. Alec's immaculate left foot became worth its weight in gold, as he made passes with almost uncanny accuracy. As he stayed in the side, so did his assurance become more obvious, and he made an increasing contribution to the attacking power of the team, as well as being a stout defender. He also became a deadly marksman from the penalty spot, and in the summer of 1974 his all-round ability won him recognition, for he was selected to play for England, although later he found himself out of the first-team limelight at Anfield.

Steve Heighway seen during training at Anfield. Heighway scored one of Liverpool's three goals in the 1974 Cup Final.

Mention of England brings us to Emlyn Hughes, who grew in stature after his transfer from Blackpool to Liverpool to the point where he captained the International side. Emlyn, the son of a Rugby International, had played but a handful of first-team games for Blackpool when Shankly signed him for £65 000. As time went by, and he became established in midfield for Liverpool, the arguments grew because England team manager Sir Alf Ramsey picked Emlyn at left-back. Emlyn himself admitted at the start that he enjoyed going forward most – nothing pleased him better than to move upfield, then cut in from the left and send a shot screaming for goal. However, as time went by, he became an integral part of Liverpool's back-four line, too, when a team reshuffle became necessary. He attained the captaincy of Liverpool, and never lost that surging enthusiasm which took him past opponents and drove his own team-mates on to victory. More than 500 games and close on half a century of goals for his club help to demonstrate Emlyn's success in top-class football, even if, after Don Revie's arrival on the scene as England team manager, Hughes had to suffer the disappointment of losing his International place.

Alun Evans became the first teenager to cost a £100 000 transfer fee, when he joined Liverpool from Wolves in September, 1968. The flaxen-haired youngster of eighteen made his mark with a goal on his debut against

Brian Hall seen during his own 'Chat Show' on B.B.C. Radio Merseyside.

Leicester. There were other occasions when he won the cheers of the crowd – a hat-trick in a European tie, and the goal in the 1971 semi-final which set Liverpool on the way to Wembley. Evans was a player who could show flashes of brilliant opportunism, but there were also times when he was in the shadows at Anfield, and in June, 1972, he returned to the Midlands, signed by Aston Villa for £80 000.

In contrast to the costly fees paid for Evans, Steve Heighway was signed by Liverpool from Skelmersdale United, who at the time were a Cheshire League club. Heighway, a high-stepping and fleet-footed left-winger with a flair for scoring spectacular goals, had interested more than one club, but as well as playing for 'Skem', he was also completing his studies at Warwick University, where he graduated as a Bachelor of Arts. Liverpool manager Bill Shankly talked to him, and persuaded him to try his luck at professional football. In his first full season Heighway became a member of Liverpool's FA Cup-final team.

His was a remarkable rise to stardom; and perhaps the way things happened so quickly left him a bit bewildered. But the fact remained that he was ready to try unorthodox moves which caught out defenders and although he started out thinking that success would be transitory, he became a regular member of the first team, collecting medals in the League and the UEFA Cup, and returning to Wembley as a member of the 1974 Cup-winning side.

Brian Hall was another university graduate who became a professional footballer with Liverpool. He is a Bachelor of Science, and the night Heighway made his debut in a League Cup-tie against Mansfield, Hall was also in the side. Hall plays in midfield, and his tenacious approach to the game, combined with his agility, make him a player who never gives up. The £115 000 signing of Scotland International Peter Cormack from Nottingham Forest, in 1972, curtailed Hall's first-team appearances for a while, but he came back to play a part in Liverpool's Wembley success of 1974.

It was Hall who scored the semi-final winner against Everton at Old Trafford, in 1971, and he has now played well over 200 games for Liverpool, while Heighway has passed the 300 mark by a considerable margin. Cormack, like Hall and Heighway, has shared in Liverpool's achievements of the 1970s, and he has stolen some vital goals for the club. So has Phil Boersma (now with Middlesborough), who scored his first hat-trick in First Division football when Liverpool demolished Tottenham at the start of season 1974-5.

Boersma was in the side for a long, unbroken run, as Liverpool caned Spurs 5-2, and it must have been a sweet taste of success for Boersma, as he heard the roar of the crowd, because only a few months earlier he had made his way from Wembley dejected at having failed to land even the substitute's place in Liverpool's FA Cup-final team. The substitute that day was Chris Lawler, who had been out of action for a lengthy period because of a cartilage operation.

When it comes to goals, mention must be made of John Toshack, of course, who was signed by Liverpool from Cardiff for £110 000 in 1970. This tall Welsh International, like Boersma, has had his out-of-form patches during his career at Anfield, but he has certainly made his presence felt, especially with his ability to win the ball in the air, and his scoring record is a tribute to his consistent marksmanship. In just over 400 games he has scored close on 170 goals; and included in that figure are more than 80 for Liverpool, in just over 200 appearances. Toshack's claim to a regular first-team place was in some jeopardy with the £200 000 signing of Ray Kennedy from Arsenal, but so far as Liverpool were concerned, it meant that they had an increasingly strong first-team pool of players, even though Larry Lloyd had departed for

Wembley 1974. Keegan scores a brilliant goal for Liverpool. Liverpool won the match 3–0.

Ray Kennedy signed from Arsenal for the 1974-5 season.

John Toshack, Liverpool's most brilliant goal scorer.

Kevin Keegan photographed by team mate Alec Lindsay during a flight to a European match.

Coventry and brought Liverpool their record fee of £240 000. Now Toshack and Keegan form an almost inseparable, dynamic goal-scoring duo, and Kennedy has blossomed as a midfield player who has been capped by England while other newcomers such as Phil Neal, Jimmy Case and David Fairclough have made their mark.

Larry Lloyd was another who missed the 1974 FA Cup final after having dropped out earlier through injury, and a team reshuffle saw some players swtiched around, and a new face in the side. With Lawler out, Smith moved to right back, and Hughes became a regular back-four player, alongside a lanky beanpole of a youngster, Phil Thompson, who had himself started out as a midfield player. Thompson emerged as another star of the Anfield firmament who kept his place at Wembley, where the Liverpool line-up was as follows: Clemence, Smith, Lindsay, Thompson, Cormack, Hughes, Keegan, Hall, Heighway, Toshack, Callaghan.

In the final against Newcastle, Liverpool exuded confidence from the kick-off, and although Newcastle managed to survive for a considerable time without conceding a goal, there rarely appeared to be any doubt about the eventual outcome as Liverpool subjected the Magpies to ever-increasing pressure. Two goals from Kevin Keegan and one from Heighway settled matters, and Malcolm Macdonald rarely had a chance to get in a worthwhile scoring effort during the whole ninety minutes. Keegan, the player who had zoomed from Soccer in the lower divisions with Scunthorpe to England International status, buzzed like a hornet, and proved for the umpteenth time that, at £35 000, he had been a snip of a purchase. And the seal was set on his career, when at the end of season 1975-6, he was named by the sportswriters as the Footballer of the Year.

All in all, it was a team performance of which Liverpool could indeed be proud, for they dominated the final, especially in the second half. If there was any disappointment, it must have been that Newcastle – self-admittedly – did not play up to their pre-match promise. However, that does not detract from the fact that Liverpool displayed some flowing football as they set about Newcastle, who for long spells could do little more than hang on grimly. When it was all over, nobody could begrudge Liverpool their triumph, and it was a seething, happy mass of Liverpool supporters who conga'd their way from the famous stadium, chanting in their joy: 'We've all been to Wembley! We've all been to Wembley!'

MIDLAND BANK
DAILY MIRROR

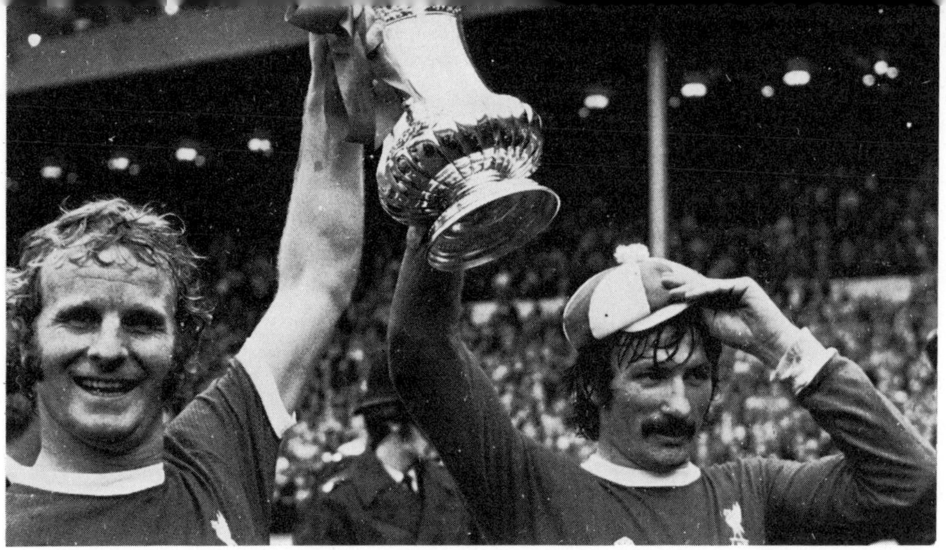

Kevin Keegan collects the ball on the edge of the penalty area and blasts home Liverpool's first goal in the 1974 FA Cup Final (page 74).

Tommy Smith, Alec Lindsay and Ray Clemence display the FA Cup after their 1974 Wembley triumph (page 74).

Lindsay and Smith after the 1974 victory (above).

Shankly – and two worshippers – after the 1974 FA Cup victory.

So, in three trips to the final inside a ten-year period, Liverpool had carried off the FA Cup on two occasions. The team of the 1970s, with the League Championship and the UEFA Cup also among their list of credits, had cast off the shadow of their predecessors who achieved so much glory during the 1960s. The 'new' Liverpool had unfurled its banner; the players had come of age, and no longer did they require any reassurance from anyone that they could measure up to the best. They had indeed earned their laurels, and their deeds spoke for them.

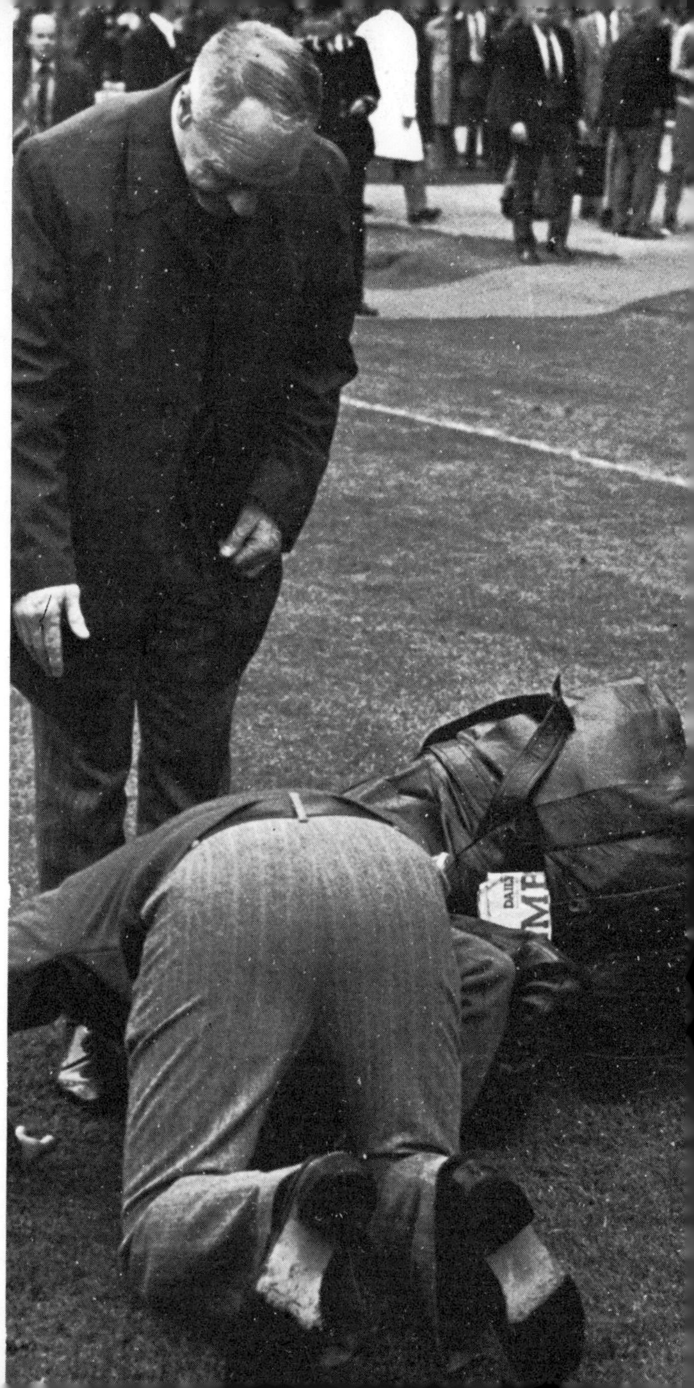

7 The Continental Safari

When Liverpool met Borussia Mönchengladbach at Anfield on the night of Wednesday, 9 May, 1973, they were playing their sixty-fifth game of the season since kick-off day on 12 August, 1972. It had been a gruelling fixture list, but Liverpool had come through to capture the First Division Championship and in their match against Borussia they were only 180 minutes away from taking their first European trophy, the UEFA Cup. Liverpool scored three goals without reply, and in the second leg, in Germany, they survived a battering and restricted their opponents – Günter Netzer and all – to two goals, so that the UEFA Cup was won on a 3-2 aggregate. The trophy travelled back with Liverpool as they flew home through the night. It had been a long wait, but worth it.

Nine seasons of striving for a European trophy began on 17 August, 1964, when Liverpool entered the European Cup and travelled to Reykjavik, in Iceland. It was the start of a trail which was to take Liverpool through many countries: Belgium, Germany (East and West), Italy, Hungary, Rumania, Holland, Sweden, Spain, Portugal, Switzerland, Greece, Luxembourg, Norway, Poland and Yugoslavia. Liverpool had competed previously in the Friendship Cup, and had met Nântes in season 1960-1. The start of their quest for European honours, however, really began with that game against Reykjavik, which they won 5-0.

In the return game Liverpool scored six goals at Anfield, while conceding one, and the next round pitched them into battle against the top Belgian club, Anderlecht. Liverpool duly triumphed again, winning 3-0 at Anfield and 1-0 away, and so they tackled Cologne. Neither side could manage a goal, in either leg, and after a play-off in Rotterdam, the score was 2-2. It was Liverpool who, on the flip of a coin, went through to meet the mighty Inter-Milan in the semi-finals. That was a tie which was to produce one of the glorious nights at Anfield and leave Liverpool smarting from a sense of injustice about what happened in Milan.

Inter came, saw – and were conquered at Anfield. Liverpool wasted no time on frivolities; they stuck three goals past Inter, while conceding one. It seemed as if the Anfield Reds were in a fair position to knock Inter-Milan off the

Tommy Smith on a flight to a European match with a cake given to the team for good luck.

European Cup trail and enter the final themselves. But fate played Liverpool some scurvy tricks in the return match and the Italian team won 3-0. There were refereeing decisions which went against Liverpool, and they returned home feeling that they had been robbed.

Almost from the moment that they set foot in Italy, Liverpool were subjected to the pressures which, the fanatical Italian supporters hoped, would have them buckling at the knees even before a ball had been kicked. Players who took part in that game still recall with a shudder how two of the goals should never have been allowed, in their opinion – one came from an indirect free-kick, another when the ball was kicked from the hands of goalkeeper Tommy Lawrence. Ian Callaghan still talks about that night as one of the most disappointing in his career.

However, Liverpool had to accept the decisions, and they returned home sick at heart. Yet such was their resilience that they plunged into the Cup-winners' Cup competition the following season and went all the way to the final. They lost their first-round game in Italy 1-0, against Juventus, but scored two goals without reply at Anfield. They beat Standard Liège of

Belgium 3-1 at home and 2-1 away, and they drew, 0-0, against Honved in Hungary and beat them 2-0 in Liverpool. Then there was a semi-final against a British club, Glasgow Celtic, and Liverpool survived a 1-0 defeat in Scotland, to rap back with two goals on their own ground. So, on 5 May, 1966, Liverpool went into their first European final, against Borussia Dortmund, at Hampden Park, Glasgow.

By Liverpool's own admission, it was not a classic game, and they did not do themselves justice. Two of their players scored that night, and Held got a goal for Borussia. Roger Hunt was the marksman for Liverpool; unfortunately, the goal which big Ron Yeats scored counted against the Reds, for it was put past his own 'keeper, Tommy Lawrence.

The following season, Liverpool had another tilt at the European Cup, the most glittering prize on the Continental circuit. They were drawn in the first round against a Rumanian side, Petrolul Ploesti, and they knew they had a tough opponent to conquer, but conquer they did, with a 2-0 victory at Anfield, and they stayed in the hunt on the strength of their lone goal in Rumania, although they conceded three in the away game. For that goal gave them a play-off in Brussels, and this time Liverpool had little opposition, scoring goals by Ian St John and Peter Thompson.

Now Liverpool were up against Ajax, from Holland, but this knowledge did not deter them. They believed they could give a good account of themselves, even though the first leg was an away game. That game turned out to be a disaster for Liverpool, who failed to take the initiative. Ajax were a team who gave no quarter, as they hammered five goals past Liverpool, who could manage only one in reply, from Chris Lawler. Liverpool had been set a daunting task at Anfield, but the Kop and the rest of the fans gave them every support. You could even have been forgiven for thinking that Liverpool were the team who had the edge from the first game.

Even so, and bravely as Liverpool fought, their hopes were damned. They scored two goals – but so did Ajax. And once more, Liverpool were out of Europe, although grimly determined to try again the following season. Sure enough, they did, by virtue of their displays in the First Division, which won them a place in the Fairs Cup. Victories over the Swedish club, Malmo – 2-0 away and 2-1 at Anfield – brought them up against the German side, Munich 1860, and it was in the home game that Liverpool ran riot. They swept to victory, rattling in eight goals, to kill the tie as a contest. Somewhat surprisingly, Munich were the victors in the second leg, by 2-1, but it was a result which was of no real consequence, as Liverpool marched on to meet the Hungarians of Ferencvaros.

The Hungarians were a hard side to beat; they, too, had had plenty of experience in European competition, and they showed their mettle by becoming the first side from the Continent to win at Anfield. Ferencvaros arrived at Anfield with a single-goal lead from the first leg; they repeated their performance and thrust Liverpool off the European trail. The following season, it was the Spanish club, Bilbao, who created problems for the Liverpool team, for they finished level on aggragate in the first round of the Fairs Cup. Liverpool lost 2-1 in Bilbao ... then gained a meritorious victory by the same margin on their own ground. But this time the flip of a disc gave Bilbao the right to go through to the next round.

In season 1969-70, Liverpool inspired confidence when they scored their record victory – 10-0 – at Anfield against the League of Ireland side, Dundalk, and they followed up with a four-goal victory in the away game. This was at the time when the old Liverpool side was being broken up, and the newcomers were beginning to prove their ability. Although it was still a time of transition, Liverpool could count themselves unfortunate indeed to fail to get beyond the second round when they came up against the Portuguese team, Vitoria Setubal.

Many people had regarded this tie as being a mere formality for Liverpool; their opponents were not well known in this country, and it was thought Liverpool would master them. The first leg was in Portugal, and Liverpool returned confident they could overcome the handicap of being only one goal behind. But on the night of the second leg, at Anfield, Vitoria Setubal showed that they, too, were made of stern stuff, and although Liverpool scored three times, Setubal managed a couple of goals themselves. The Liverpool fans rose in their seats, at the final whistle, thinking that, at the last gasp, their heroes had done sufficient to remain in the tournament. Then there was hesitation, and finally, as the crowd listened in silence, it was announced that Vitoria Setubal would go through, because of the fact that their away goals counted double, as the game had ended in an aggregate draw. Liverpool had battled mightily, and they had conquered – but they had to admit that it would have been just as hard on Setubal, had the situation been reversed, for the Portuguese had certainly made it a memorable match.

Cormack and Keegan photographed by the Danube in Budapest.

Toshack, Lawler and Lloyd applaud Alun Evans' second goal against Bayern Munich in March 1971.

Once again, in season 1970-1, Liverpool went into the Fairs Cup. It was their seventh successive campaign in European competition, and they had high hopes that this time they would finish with a trophy to show for their efforts. Their first opponents were Ferencvaros, and on this occasion Liverpool triumphed, winning 1-0 at Anfield and drawing the return, 1-1, with a display of resolute football. Dinamo Bucharest came next, and they were virtually despatched from the competition in the first leg at Anfield, which Liverpool won 3-0. Dinamo's 1-1 draw in Bucharest did not matter, and Liverpool had a relatively comfortable task in the third round, when they met Scottish club Hibernian. Liverpool had one or two frights, but they never looked like losers, and they won 1-0 in Edinburgh and 2-0 at Anfield.

Now the heat was on, for Liverpool's next opponents were Bayern Munich, who had the great Franz Beckenbauer and Gerd Müller to inspire them. The first leg was at Anfield. It was memorable for the fact that Alun Evans scored a hat-trick for Liverpool, and for the fact, also, that Bayern never really posed much of a threat – indeed, that was almost as much of a talking point as the Evans hat-trick. Bayern were expected to be much more of a menace on their own ground, and some faint hearts even wondered if that three-goal lead would be whittled away. However, on the night, Bayern could do no better than draw 1-1, and so Liverpool took on an even stiffer task when they matched themselves against Leeds, in the semi-final.

As ever, Liverpool and Leeds fought doggedly and neither gave nor sought quarter. It was, from the start, a game which could go either way – and it went Leeds United's way at Anfield, in the first leg. When Liverpool travelled to Elland Road they were trailing by a goal, and although they tried to live up to their manager's brave words, 'the tie's not over, yet', they had to be content with a no-score draw, and so they were out of the competition just as they had reached the verge of success. There was a sense of disappointment, too, about their venture into the Cup-winners' Cup in season 1971-2, for they made hard work of disposing of Servette, an unrated team from Geneva. Liverpool lost the away game 2-1, and settled the result only by scoring two goals without reply at Anfield. Altogether not a convincing start to the campaign.

Hopes were raised when Liverpool drew Bayern Munich again, in the second round. The Anfield faithful recalled the last meeting between the clubs, and were optimistic that Bayern would suffer a similar fate. This time unfortunately, it was Liverpool who fell; they could not score one goal in the Anfield game, and they lost the away match 3-1. They were then at the end of their eighth season in succession in Europe, and one game short of half a century in competition against the Continentals. True, they had never managed to collect a trophy; but their record was pretty good. Liverpool had played 49 games, won 25 and drawn 10. They had scored 90 goals, and conceded 43. Had there been points for victories and draws, they would have totalled 60 out of a possible 98.

Thus dawned the season of 1972-3, with Liverpool competing not in the Fairs Cup, but the renamed UEFA Cup. By then, the 'new' team had settled in, and individual players were forecasting that they must surely win some trophy or other. Liverpool had been to Wembley in the FA Cup and lost, against Arsenal, and they had only just failed to gain the First Division title. There was a feeling akin to that of conviction, yet lingering fear, as if the 1972-3 season was the testing time, the season that would make or break. As it turned out, it was a season which made Liverpool, for not only did they win the Championship of the First Division, they carried off the UEFA Cup, as well.

John Toshack who has contributed to so much of Liverpool successes in Europe.

Liverpool walk out to their match with AEK in Athens in September 1972.

The story of that Championship season is told elsewhere; this is the place to detail the events which led to Liverpool winning the UEFA Cup. It all began at Anfield on the night of Tuesday, 12 September, 1972, when Liverpool met Eintracht Frankfurt. Memories were stirred as people recalled that European Cup final in Glasgow between Eintracht and Real Madrid, when Real pumped seven goals past the Germans, and conceded three themselves in a game which was a classic. Perhaps some people felt that Eintracht might produce the same magical play against Liverpool at Anfield, but the giants of the past had faded. Liverpool won comfortably, 2-0, and dispelled any fears of a shock defeat by drawing no-score in the away leg. Even then, there was no hint of the drama still to be played, not even when Liverpool beat AEK of Athens, 3-0 at Anfield and 3-1 in Greece.

From Athens, Liverpool travelled behind the Iron Curtain, where they met and mastered Dynamo Berlin, drawing 0-0 in the away leg and winning the Anfield game 3-1. Then they returned to meet another team called Dynamo – the East German Dynamo Dresden – and they really proved to be tough opposition. In fact, Bill Shankly rated Liverpool's performances against them as two of the club's best, in Europe. Liverpool won the Anfield game 2-0, but there were suspicions that even this margin might not be sufficient to take the Reds through; in Dresden, however, Liverpool raised their game magnificently, and scored the only goal of the match.

So Liverpool were through to the semi-finals – and up against the team which, the previous season, had beaten Wolves in the final to take the UEFA Cup. The holders were Tottenham Hotspur, who had had some fine duels with Liverpool in the past; and now these two magnificent English clubs were rivals once again, this time for a trophy in Europe. The first game was played at Anfield, and Spurs threatened more than once to steal a goal; but Liverpool prevented this happening, and they scored one themselves to go into the return holding the slenderest of leads. Again, it seemed that this lone goal would not be sufficient, and at White Hart Lane Spurs must have anticipated holding on to the trophy because they scored, and scored again. Yet Liverpool are nothing, if not dauntless, and it was Steve Heighway who put the ball into the Spurs net to see Liverpool through to the final, because that away goal counted double.

If the game at White Hart Lane had had the spectators sizzling with excitement, the final itself was to prove worthy of the occasion, and you needed a strong heart to be able to stand the strain. Liverpool had the good fortune to meet Borussia Mönchengladbach at Anfield in the first leg, and they set upon their West German opponents as if to settle matters there and then. The final score was Liverpool 3, Borussia Mönchengladbach 0. And it seemed as if the trophy was in the bag for the Anfield men, who travelled to Mönchengladbach filled with confidence that nothing would disrupt their plans for a triumphant return.

Several thousand British Servicemen stationed in Germany went to the game to lend their support to Liverpool; but even so, the stadium was thronged with people who were predominantly German fans, and the noise throughout the game was deafening, especially so when Borussia forged ahead with a two-goal lead. It was the reverse of what had happened at Anfield, and this time it was Liverpool who were hanging grimly on to the ropes, like a boxer who keeps taking punches but, somehow, is kept on his feet by instinct alone. Few teams have rocked Liverpool back on their heels as did the German side, powered from midfield by Günter Netzer. It became a question of whether or not Liverpool could hold on without conceding yet another goal, before half-time had arrived. They did hold on, but there was foreboding among the British contingent as to what disasters might befall in the second half.

Heaven, they say, helps those who help themselves. In the second half Liverpool came out determined to do just that. They were brave, and they were lucky. As the minutes ticked away with agonising slowness, it began to dawn upon players and spectators alike that here was a last-ditch stand which might – just might – prove successful. The German players began to sense it, and their efforts bordered on the anxious; and the Liverpool players began to sense it, too. As the game slowly ticked towards its finish, they began to sneak back into the picture, with one or two raids which had the Germans afraid of being caught on the break and conceding a goal themselves. Liverpool, while never dominating, began to grow in assurance as they realised that their opponents' confidence was being shredded, and replaced with taut anxiety.

Liverpool survived the final Borussia assault, and the game was over. The Reds had held their line, and the UEFA Cup was theirs. In the dressing-room players were pale-faced – even Bill Shankly's face told of the strain. Words were at a premium, too, for a time; the players had literally left themselves breathless. It was a tremendous achievement, and as the players boarded

Heighway's second goal against Dynamo Berlin in 1972.

their coach for the airport and the night flight back to Liverpool, laughter began to peal and jokes were cracked, now that the tension had eased. Over the radio came the strains of the British national anthem; it seemed so appropriate.

Liverpool fans thronged the entrance to the airport, but it was nothing compared with the scene when the plane touched down at Speke around 2.30 the next morning. Thousands of supporters were waiting for a glimpse of their heroes, and they swept across the apron to the plane and simply surrounded it. Bill Shankly and his players were taken aback, and it was a while before they could reach the comparative peace of the customs hall. So Liverpool had carved themselves another piece of football history by becoming the first English club to capture the League Championship and a European trophy in the same season. They had played 66 competitive games and shown what could be done.

The following season they were back in Europe again, this time in the European Cup, and after disposing of Jeunesse D'Esch, of Luxembourg (1-1 away, 2-0 at Anfield), they took on Red Star Belgrade, managed by Miljan Miljanic who was later to take over Real Madrid after steering Yugoslavia to the 1974 World Cup finals. Liverpool met defeat in Belgrade, for they lost 2-1,

Keen photographer Alec Lindsay takes pictures of his team-mates during a flight to Oslo.

Emlyn Hughes leads out the Liverpool team in their match against Ferencvaros at Budapest in November 1974.

and although they felt confident about turning the tables at Anfield, it was not to be. Red Star, who had said they would not bring men merely to defend, scored two goals once more, to Liverpool's one. So another European sortie was over; but at least Liverpool had the consolation of taking the FA Cup to Anfield that season; and they had qualified for Europe, in the Cup-winners' Cup, to take their unbroken run to eleven seasons.

A home victory by an 11-0 record margin over the Norwegians of Stromsgodset fanned Liverpool hopes of a Cup-winner's Cup triumph in Bob Paisley's first season as manager, and Liverpool, as anticipated, also won the return – but only by 1-0. This meant that in the second round, Liverpool came up against their old adversaries from Hungary, Ferencvaros, and the scoreline of 1-1 at the end of the first leg at Anfield caused some fears for Liverpool's survival. Those fears were not unfounded, because while Liverpool drew a scoreless second leg in Hungary, they went out on the strength of that goal which Ferencvaros had scored at Anfield. Since the teams had drawn on aggregate, it counted double.

By finishing as runners-up in the First Division Championship, however, Liverpool embarked upon their twelfth successive season of European competition, when season 1975-6 came around, and once more it was the UEFA Cup, in which they had triumphed in 1973. The first leg of the first round was against Hibernian, at Easter Road, and Hibs won, 1-0. A hat-trick from John Toshack, however – his first for Liverpool – gave the Anfield men a 3-1 victory in the return, and enabled Toshack to chalk up a career total of 150 goals, in the process.

After Scottish opposition, Liverpool had to play in Spain, and they met Real Sociedad in San Sebastian, and scored a 3-1 victory. In the return match at Anfield, Liverpool doubled that tally, without conceding a goal. When they played their next tie, the winter had come, and in contrast to the sunshine of Spain. Liverpool travelled to find snow on the ground in Poland, when they met Slask Wroclaw. The pitch was tricky, with its frozen layer, yet Liverpool demonstrated that they were both skilled and brave, and they emerged the victors by 2-1. At Anfield, they beat Slask Wroclaw again, this time by a 3-0 margin, as Jimmy Case scored a hat-trick.

Perhaps it was an omen, when Liverpool were paired with Dynamo Dresden in the quarter-finals, for it was Dynamo whom they had met, at the same stage of the competition, when they had conquered and gone on to win

The Norwegian team Stromsgodset were soundly thrashed by Liverpool in September 1974, but did not lose their sense of humour as these cartoons drawn by the Norwegian's Club Supporters show.

the trophy three years earlier. This time, Dynamo were thought to be an even better side than when they had met Liverpool previously; but the first leg in Dresden ended scoreless, to give Liverpool confidence for the return.

The second leg still remained to be won, however, and Liverpool did not have things all their own way; but they struck twice, while Dynamo managed only one goal, and that took them into the semi-finals. The big question then was whether Liverpool would be drawn against FC Bruges, SV Hamburg – or the glamour club Barcelona, who had world-class stars Johan Neeskens and Johan Cruyff playing for them. Cruyff had played against Liverpool before, in his days with Ajax; and by a further twist of fate, the man in charge of Barcelona was Hennes Weisweiler, who had managed Borussia Moenchengladbach when they met Liverpool in the 1973 final. Many people felt that Barcelona was the one club Liverpool wanted to avoid – if they had to tangle with the star-studded Spanish team, better the final than the penultimate stage of the competition. But Liverpool, like beggars, couldn't be choosers, and the draw paired them against Cruyff and company. Before the first leg, which was in Spain, Cruyff expressed the opinion that he would not be really happy unless Barcelona secured a two-goal lead. His hopes were dashed, when John Toshack struck a goal early in the game, and Liverpool played superbly to snuff out the danger of any reply from Barcelona.

Barcelona played well – that was beyond dispute; but on the night, Liverpool played even better. And when the scoreline still stood at 1-0 in favour of Liverpool at the end of 90 minutes, the 70 000 fans in the stadium recognised that the damage had probably been done. Cushions rained down on the pitch, as if to emphasise their disappointment at the result, so far as Barcelona were concerned. And Weisweiler resigned his job. Once again, however, the battle was not over, and Barcelona arrived at Anfield in the mood to show that they could still pose a threat. When Phil Thompson scored for Liverpool, the issue seemed to be settled; but inside a minute or so, a flash of magic from Cruyff, on the left, paved the way for Barcelona to hit back with a swift counter, and the game was still wide open. Liverpool might be winning 2-1, but if Barcelona managed just one more goal, and prevented Liverpool from scoring again, they would go through to the final on aggregate, because their away goals would count double. Liverpool, however, kept their heads and their overall lead, and it was Barcelona who tropped dejectedly off the field. In the other semi-final, Bruges had got the better of Hamburg.

Liverpool met Bruges, the Belgian Champions, in the first leg of the final at Anfield on 28 April, 1976. In front of almost 50 000 spectators (including an estimated 2500 fans from Belgium) Liverpool conceded two goals early in the match and they were still trailing 0-2 at half-time. When the teams walked out for the second half of the match the familiar figure of John Toshack was missing – Jimmy Case had been sent on as substitute. Once again Liverpool demonstrated their amazing resilience, fought back with goals by Kennedy and Case and clinched a narrow victory when Keegan scored from the penalty spot. In the second leg of the UEFA final at Bruges on 19 May a one-all draw (Keegan scored for Liverpool) ensured that the UEFA Cup went to Anfield for the second time.

Keegan is seen during the match with Ferencvaros in November 1974.

Keegan after scoring in the first leg of the match with Ferencvaros at Anfield in 1974.

Boersma congratulates Heighway after the latter has score in a European match against Hibernian.

First Division Match

EVERTON v. LIVERPOOL

AT GOODISON PARK. KICK-OFF 3-15 p.m.

Right. EVERTON Left.

1 SAGAR
2 WILLIAMS 3 CRESSWELL
4 BRITTON 5 WHITE 6 THOMSON
7 CRITCHLEY 8 McGOURTY 9 DEAN 10 JOHNSON 11 STEIN

C

GUNSON 12 McPHERSON 13 WRIGHT 14 HODGSON 15 BARTON 16
McDOUGALL 17 BRADSHAW 18 MORRISON 19
JACKSON 20 STEEL 21
SCOTT 22

Left. LIVERPOOL Right

Referee: Mr. H. E. HULL (Burnley)
Linesmen: J. W. TILSTON (Blue and White Flag).
T. TALBOT (Red and White Flag).

N.B. Teams subject to alteration. Changes will be announced from the Loud Speaker.

Central League Match.

Liverpool Res. v. Everton Res.

AT ANFIELD. KICK-OFF 3-15 p.m.

Right. LIVERPOOL RES. Left.

1 RILEY
2 DONE 3 LUCAS
4 SAVAGE 5 JAMES 6 HENDERSON
7 McRORIE 8 HANCOCK 9 CRAWFORD 10 ROBERTS 11 TAYLOR

C

TURNER 12 WEBSTER 13 STEVENS 14 CUNLIFFE 15 GRIFFITHS, P. H. 16
MERCER 17 GRIFFITHS, H. S. 18 ARCHER 19
LOWE 20 COMMON 21
COGGINS 22

Left. EVERTON RES. Right

Referee: Mr. C. W. ABBOTT (Sheffield).
Linesmen: N. ORMROD (Red Striped Flag).
W. RYAN (Blue Striped Flag).

N.B. Teams subject to alteration. Changes will be sent round the ground on the board

8 The Day of the Derby

Local derby games between Liverpool and Everton have been going on, season by season, since 1894. The first meeting of the two great rivals took place at Goodison Park on 13 October of that year, and since then there have been more than 100 derby games. The first attracted a crowd of 44 000 people, but both Anfield and Goodison these days stage full-house derby games which draw around 55 000 spectators. In addition to derby clashes in the League, Liverpool have met Everton 11 times is the FA Cup. Up to the start of season 1976-7, Liverpool and Everton had met 114 times in League games, and the balance of power has been fairly even – Liverpool having won 38 times against Everton's 43 victories, with the remaining 33 matches drawn. At Anfield, Liverpool have won 22 of the games, lost 19 and drawn 16; at Goodison, they have won 16, lost 24 and drawn 17 games.

Liverpool's biggest home victories have been 6-0 (September, 1935), 7-4 (February, 1933), 5-1 (October, 1922 and September, 1925), 5-0 (September 1965), and 4-0 (April, 1948 and March, 1972). At Goodison they scored their greatest victories with these results: 4-2 (October, 1907) and 3-0 (October, 1920, September, 1947 and December, 1969). The FA Cup clashes between Liverpool and Everton produced these results, up to season 1976-7: 1902 – Liverpool 2, Everton 2, with Liverpool winning the replay 2-0; 1905 – Liverpool 1, Everton 1, with Liverpool losing the replay away, 1-2; 1906 – semi-final at Villa Park, Liverpool 0, Everton 2; 1911 – Everton 2, Liverpool 1; 1932 – Everton 1, Liverpool 2; 1950 – semi-final at Maine Road, Liverpool 2, Everton 0; 1954 – Everton 0, Liverpool 4; 1967 – Everton 1, Liverpool 0.

Certainly the derby game which caused the most excitement was the 1971 FA Cup semi-final battle between Liverpool and Everton at Old Trafford, when Liverpool snatched victory after seeming to be on the way to defeat. In recent years Everton perhaps have not played with the conviction of their rivals when the teams have met, but at Old Trafford it was Everton who started off as if they intended to dominate the game, and it came as little surprise when they scored first, through Alan Ball.

However, Liverpool put up a determined performance, and although they were aided by luck, when an injury to Everton's centre-half, Brian Labone, forced him to limp out of the game, the Reds came back with that well-known fighting spirit which, eventually, gave them the right to go to Wembley. Sandy Brown replaced Labone as substitute, and Everton fought gamely, right to the end. However, Liverpool, having changed their tactics in the second half, sensed that victory could be achieved, and goals from Alun Evans and Brian Hall did the trick.

One of the enduring memories from that game is of the after-match scenes in the corridors of Old Trafford. The Liverpool players, naturally, were all smiles; but when the Everton players trooped dejectedly from their dressing-room, it was clear that several of them were on the verge of shedding tears. Most of them looked somewhat stunned, as if still unable to believe that the game had not gone their way, after they had forged a first-half lead and looked on top. Neutral observers, while not denying Liverpool's right to victory in the end, could not conceal their sympathy for Everton's players, because they were obviously feeling the blow so keenly.

Mostly, players who have worn the colours of one or other of the great Merseyside clubs have owed allegiance to no others, or have moved to clubs a considerable distance away when they have departed. Only a few have had the distinction of playing for both Liverpool and Everton, and they must surely have had mixed emotions, at various times, when the local derby games have come round. In the early days there was the Irish International Billy Lacey, who won ten caps with Everton and thirteen as a Liverpool player, and since then there have been a few other names at both Anfield and Goodison. Liverpool signed Tommy Johnson, Tony McNamara and Dave Hickson from Everton; and Ted Forshaw, Jimmy Payne and Johnny Morrissey 'crossed the park' to play for the Goodison club.

Liverpool have set many records from the days of the distant past to modern times. For instance, they had a run of 31 games without defeat when the club was first founded, and this record stood for 75 years until Leeds United claimed the record with a run of 34 games unbeaten in seasons 1968-9 and 1969-70. In March, 1973, Liverpool set a new club record for victories when they defeated Norwich City and thus gained their thirty-second win of the season, to beat the 31 victories achieved in season 1965-6. In season 1975-6, too, they claimed 33 victories during a 59-match Campaign at home and in Europe.

Everton Captain Brian Labone and Liverpool Captain Ron Yeats at the 100th game between Everton and Liverpool at Anfield in October 1968.

Larry Lloyd after the Liverpool v. Everton FA Cup Semi-Final, March 1971.

On the field and off it, Liverpool have claims to fame. They have topped the million mark for attendances in League matches at Anfield during a season; they have one of the finest grounds in the country, and this includes facilities for televising football matches. Indeed, the BBC's first *Match of the Day* programme was screened from Anfield, and Liverpool was also the setting for the first colour showing of that programme. Liverpool's floodlighting system, which cost around £50 000, is one of the best in the world, as the television technicians happily concede, and many times in the past decade Liverpool's home games against European opponents have been referred to as 'Anfield nights.' There has been colour, glamour and excitement to charge the atmosphere, and television has often captured this for millions of viewers at home and abroad.

Liverpool, rightly, have won an extraordinary reputation for near-invincibility at Anfield. It is always something of a shock when a team wins there, as Arsenal did in seasons 1972-3 and 1973-4, and as Norwich and Middlesbrough did in 1975-6, Liverpool won all their home League matches – fifteen of them – in their first season, and they have won promotion at the first attempt on no fewer than three occasions. Up to season 1975-6, if there has been one competition which has posed problems for Liverpool, it has been the Football League Cup, for they have never reached even the semi-final stages of this tournament, while gaining nine First Division Championships and winning the FA Cup twice in five final appearances.

Anfield has also staged four FA Cup semi-finals, the last one as far back as 1929. Possibly the fact that Liverpool themselves so often seem to be concerned with the later stages of the FA Cup competition has had something to do with the fact that Anfield has not staged more semi-final games. But whatever the reason, there have been many distinguished visitors to Anfield, including Royalty.

On Saturday, 10 March, 1973, the Duke of Kent visited Liverpool's ground to unveil a plaque commemorating the rebuilding of the Anfield main stand and offices. That ceremony was the official climax to a job which had been going on for ten years, during which the club had spent more than a million pounds in its efforts to make Anfield one of the best-equipped stadiums in football. Certainly no one would dispute that this is the case.

Although bricks and mortar can look impressive, it is the people who give a football club a heart and a pulse, and through the years Liverpool Football

Club has not been short of men of vision and ability, men who gave the club stature and, not least, integrity. Such a man was 'Honest John' McKenna, an Irishman who served two terms as chairman of Liverpool FC.

McKenna had started his career as a grocer's delivery boy when he arrived on the Liverpool scene as a nineteen-year-old, and he became a wealthy man through his business acumen. He also became a leading light in the affairs of Liverpool and of football generally, for he was president of the Football League for twenty-six years, and a vice-president of the Football Association, as well as being a major figure at Liverpool. A plaque in the main entrance hall pays tribute to this man who was still giving of his best to the game when he died. It was on his way home from a meeting of the management committee that he collapsed, so he had remained 'in harness' to the end.

In later days there was another familiar figure at Anfield – Mr T.V. Williams, who became the club's president after many years of distinguished service in the cause of Liverpool. Mr Williams, one-time director and chairman, died early in 1976. He had played an important part in helping to put the club in the forefront of football. In his younger days he watched players who might be worth signing and through the years he was accorded the respect due to a man who had done so much for the club. Like McKenna, Mr Williams had also served football in a wider sense, and this, too, helped to give Liverpool prestige at home and abroad.

In recent years, two other directors have had spells as chairman, while Liverpool have collected honours. Eric Roberts was the man at the helm when Liverpool wound up the 1972-3 season with the League Championship and the UEFA Cup, and he handed over to John W. Smith, who at the end of his first season in the chair found himself bidding welcome to the guests at Liverpool's FA Cup-final banquet.

Behind the scenes, too, there has not been a more efficient secretary in football than Peter Robinson, who began his career as a seventeen-year-old 'office boy' at Stockport County, graduated to assistant secretary, became secretary successively at Crewe, Scunthrope and Brighton before succeeding the late Jimmy McInnes at Liverpool, in 1965. He has had the task of ensuring that the administrative running of the club has gone smoothly, whether it be in day-to-day routine, organising travel for trips abroad, or big-match occasions such as Cup-final and Championship celebrations.

In this Liverpool history it is impossible to recount every single name and

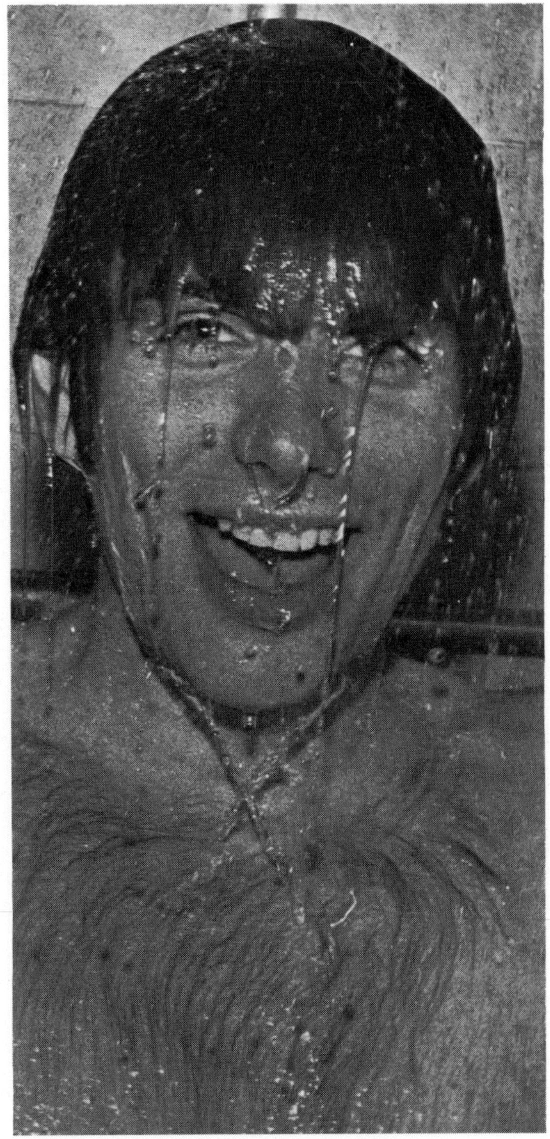

Goal scorer Alun Evans after the Liverpool v. Everton match, March 1971.

event, but it is a fact that the club has been served, in one way or another, by people who have held the highest reputations in the game, or have been merely anonymous but loyal supporters. Sir Matt Busby, for instance, was a Liverpool player before he became famous as the manager of Manchester United; and what of those thousands who, week after week, have made the trek to Anfield to stand, in one swaying, singing mass, on the slopes of the Kop?

The days have long since gone when, at the mention of Spion Kop, people thought immediately about a hillside battleground in the Boer war; and although the word Kop is applied to a particular part of any football ground in the country, when people talk about THE KOP, it is the vast throng of people who stand together behind the goal at one end of the Anfield ground which springs to mind. Liverpool's Kop has often had under its roof 24 000

Brian Hall hits the winning shot in the 1971 FA Cup Semi-Final between Liverpool and Everton.

people bound together by their devotion to the team, and it has become a unique symbol of Soccer solidarity.

Away up in the North East, where football is also something of a religion, Middlesbrough's minutes record that a player was once transferred to Darwen for £6. Middlesbrough also recorded the first £1000 transfer when they signed Alf Common from Sunderland. Like Middlesbrough, Liverpool have also hit the headlines when conducting transfer deals; in 1894 the Anfield club paid out £75 for Jimmy Ross from Preston: in 1974 they paid out £200 000 for Ray Kennedy from Arsenal. Don't times change!

Liverpool, right up to the end of the 1950s, were not noted as a 'Bank of England' club when it came to speculation in the transfer market. Indeed, until they splashed £35 000 on Ian St John, in 1961, they had not passed the £15 000 mark as buyers. It was not until 1946 that Liverpool paid their first five-figure fee – £13 000 – for Albert Stubbins, and later they also paid around £13 000 for goalkeeper Tommy Younger. It seems impossible to believe now that Gordon Milne, who shared in those great days of the 1960s, cost as little as £15 000 when he was bought from Preston. What would he have cost today?

Peter Thompson was a £40 000 buy; Emlyn Hughes and Alec Lindsay cost around £65 000 each, then came Tony Hateley, who was to move more than once for a fee of about £100 000, and Alun Evans, the £100 000 teenager. John Toshack cost £110 000 and Peter Cormack £115 000. Eventually Liverpool paid their highest-ever fee of £200 000 for Ray Kennedy.

Through the years, Liverpool have had their share of players who won International honours, but today the club can turn out an All-International line-up. These are the names of men who have worn the colours of both Liverpool and England: A'Court, Bamber, Becton, Bradshaw, Bromilow, Byrne, Callaghan, Chambers, Clemence, Cox, Hardy, Hodgson, Howell, Hughes (E.), Hughes (L.), Hunt, Jones, Keegan, Kennedy, Lawler, Lindsay, Lloyd, Longworth, Lucas, Melia, Milne, Neal, Parkinson, Smith, Taylor, Peter Thompson, Phil Thompson, and Jimmy Case is now an England under-23 player.

Many Liverpool players have also played for Scotland. You can call the roll here, too: Allan, Campbell, Cormack, Dunlop, Lawrence, Liddell, McKinlay, McNab, Miller, Morgan, Raisbeck, St John, Yeats, Younger. For Ireland there are Lacey, McMullan, Scott. Plus Heighway, of the Republic of

Ireland. And as for Wales: there have been Jones, Lambert, Latham, Matthews, Morris, Parry (E.), Parry (M.), Peake, Sidlow and Toshack.

Since 1945, something like a score of Liverpool players have won England International honours, while Billy Liddell twice played for Great Britain against the Rest of Europe. It should also be noted that Anfield itself has staged four England games, and that George Latham, Tommy Bromilow and Elisha Scott wore their respective countries' colours on the ground of their own club.

Two Liverpool players have captained England; in 1921, in Brussels, 'Eph' Longworth was the skipper against Belgium in his second International; and more than fifty years later it was the turn of Emlyn Hughes to lead out the England side, just as he leads out Liverpool.

What else is there to say about the Anfield club? It is a compliment to them that they have maintained their tradition of greatness, despite the increasing pressures of the modern game. They won their first Championship by heading the Second Division in 1894, after 28 games, and their first League-title success came in 1901, after 34 matches had been completed. In 1973, when they equalled Arsenal's feat by winning the title for the eighth time – and the UEFA Cup – Liverpool had played no fewer than 66 competitive matches that season, and won 37 of them. Ever-presents in the team were Ian Callaghan, Chris Lawler and Larry Lloyd. And in 1974, when Liverpool won the FA Cup, they played 61 competitive matches (finishing as runners-up in the League, as well, remember), and had four ever-presents: Ray Clemence, Emlyn Hughes, Ian Callaghan and Keegan. In season 1975-76, Liverpool played 59 games when they repeated their 1972-73 double, and their ever-presents were Ray Clemence and Phil Neal.

One could go on for ever emphasising individual and team achievements, for the story of Liverpool is essentially one about people. Although it has to be admitted that players come and go as the years take their toll, the club called Liverpool seems destined to remain for ever, both in the hearts of men, and as a common meeting ground for people who have a passion for the game of Soccer.

FA Cup Record

1893 – Qualifying ties: Nantwich (a) 4-0, Newton (h) 9-0, Northwich Victoria (a) 1-2
1894 – Grimsby Town (h) 3-0, Preston North End (h) 3-2, Bolton Wanderers (a) 0-3
1895 – Barnsley St Peter's (a) 1-1 and (h) 4-0, Nottingham Forest (h) 0-2
1896 – Millwall (h) 4-1, Wolves (a) 0-2
1897 – Burton Swifts (h) 4-3, West Bromwich Albion (a) 2-1, Nottingham Forest (h) 1-1 and (a) 1-0, Aston Villa (semi-final at Bramall Lane) 0-3
1898 – Hucknall St John's (h) 2-0, Newton Heath (a) 0-0 and (h) 2-1, Derby County (a) 1-1 and (h) 1-5
1899 – Blackburn Rovers (h) 2-0, Newcastle United (h) 3-1, West Bromwich Albion (a) 2-0, Sheffield United (semi-final at Nottingham) 2-2, (at Bolton) 4-4, (at Fallowfield – abandoned) 1-0, and (at Derby) 0-1
1900 – Stoke City (h) 0-0 and (a) 1-0, West Bromwich Albion (a) 1-1 and (h) 1-2
1901 – Notts. County (a) 0-2
1902 – Everton (h) 2-2 and (a) 2-0, Southampton (a) 1-4
1903 – Manchester United (a) 1-2
1904 – Blackburn Rovers (a) 1-3
1905 – Everton (h) 1-1 and (a) 1-2
1906 – Leicester Fosse (h) 2-1, Barnsley (h) 1-0, Brentford (h) 2-0, Southampton (h) 3-0, Everton (semi-final at Villa Park) 0-2
1907 – Birmingham City (h) 2-1, Oldham Athletic (a) 1-0, Bradford City (h) 1-0, Sheffield Wednesday (a) 0-1
1908 – Derby County (h) 4-2, Brighton (h) 1-1 and (a) 3-0, Newcastle United (a) 1-3
1909 – Lincoln City (h) 5-1, Norwich City (h) 2-3
1910 – Bristol City (a) 0-2
1911 – Gainsborough Trinity (h) 3-2, Everton (a) 1-2
1912 – Leyton (h) 1-0, Fulham (a) 0-3
1913 – Bristol City (h) 3-0, Woolwich Arsenal (h) 4-1, Newcastle United (h) 1-1 and (a) 0-1
1914 – Barnsley (h) 1-1 and (a) 1-0, Gillingham (h) 2-0, West Ham (a) 1-1 and (h) 5-1, Queen's Park Rangers (h) 2-1, Aston Villa (semi-final at Tottenham) 2-0, Burnley (final at Crystal Palace) 0-1
1915 – Stockport County (h) 3-0, Sheffield United (a) 0-1
1916-19 – First World War intervened

1920 – South Shields (a) 1-1 and (h) 2-0, Luton Town (a) 2-0, Birmingham City (h) 2-0, Huddersfield Town (a) 1-2
1921 – Manchester United (h) 1-1 and (a) 2-1, Newcastle United (a) 0-1
1922 – Sunderland (a) 1-1 and (h) 5-0, West Bromwich Albion (h) 0-1
1923 – Arsenal (h) 0-0 and (a) 4-1, Wolves (a) 2-0, Sheffield United (h) 1-2
1924 – Bradford City (h) 2-1, Bolton Wanderers (a) 4-1, Southampton (a) 0-0 and (h) 2-0, Newcastle United (a) 0-1
1925 – Leeds United (h) 3-0, Bristol City (a) 1-0, Birmingham City (h) 2-1, Southampton (a) 0-1
1926 – Southampton (a) 0-0 and (h) 1-0, Fulham (a) 1-3
1927 – Bournemouth (a) 1-1 and (h) 4-1, Southport (h) 3-1, Arsenal (a) 0-2
1928 – Darlington (h) 1-0, Cardiff City (a) 1-2
1929 – Bristol City (a) 2-0, Bolton Wanderers (h) 0-0 and (a) 2-5
1930 – Cardiff City (h) 1-2
1931 – Birmingham City (h) 0-2
1932 – Everton (a) 2-1, Chesterfield (a) 4-2, Grimsby Town (h) 1-0, Chelsea (h) 0-2
1933 – West Bromwich Albion (a) 0-2
1934 – Fulham (h) 1-1 and (a) 3-2, Tranmere Rovers (home – by arrangement) 3-1, Bolton Wanderers (h) 0-3
1935 – Yeovil and Petters (a) 6-2, Blackburn Rovers (a) 0-1
1936 – Swansea Town (h) 1-0, Arsenal (h) 0-2
1937 – Norwich City (a) 0-3
1938 – Crystal Palace (a) 0-0 and (h) 3-1, Sheffield United (a) 1-1 and (h) 1-0, Huddersfield Town (h) 0-1
1939 – Luton Town (h) 3-0, Stockport County (h) 5-1, Wolves (a) 1-4
1940-45 – Second World War intervened
1946 – Two-legged ties: Chester (a) 2-0 and (h) 2-1, Bolton Wanderers (a) 0-5 and (h) 2-0
1947 – Walsall (a) 5-2, Grimsby Town (h) 2-0, Derby County (h) 1-0, Birmingham City (h) 4-1, Burnley (semi-final at Ewood Park) 0-0 and (at Maine-road) 0-1
1948 – Nottingham Forest (h) 4-1, Manchester United (away – at Goodison Park) 0-3
1949 – Nottingham Forest (a) 2-2 and (h) 4-0, Notts. County (h) 1-0, Wolves (a) 1-3
1950 – Blackburn Rovers (a) 0-0 and (h) 2-1, Exeter City (h) 3-1, Stockport County (a) 2-1, Blackpool (h) 2-1, Everton (semi-final at Maine Road) 2-0, Arsenal (final at Wembley) 0-2
1951 – Norwich City (a) 1-3

1952 – Workington (h) 1-0, Wolves (h) 2-1, Burnley (a) 0-2
1953 – Gateshead (a) 0-1
1954 – Bolton Wanderers (a) 0-1
1955 – Lincoln City (a) 1-1 and (h) 1-0, Everton (a) 4-0, Huddersfield Town (h) 0-2
1956 – Accrington Stanley (h) 2-0, Scunthorpe United (h) 3-3 and (a) 2-1, Manchester City (a) 0-0 and (h) 1-2
1957 – Southend United (a) 1-2
1958 – Southend United (h) 1-1 and (a) 3-2, Northampton Town (h) 3-1, Scunthorpe United (a) 1-0, Blackburn Rovers (a) 1-2
1959 – Worcester City (a) 1-2
1960 – Leyton Orient (h) 2-1, Manchester United (h) 1-3
1961 – Coventry City (h) 3-2, Sunderland (h) 0-2
1962 – Chelsea (h) 4-3, Oldham Athletic (a) 2-1, Preston North End (h) 0-0, (a) 0-0 and (at Old Trafford) 0-1
1963 – Wrexham (a) 3-0, Burnley (a) 1-1 and (h) 2-1, Arsenal (a) 2-1, West Ham (h) 1-0, Leicester City (semi-final at Hillsborough) 0-1
1964 – Derby County (h) 5-0, Port Vale (h) 0-0 and (a) 2-1, Arsenal (a) 1-0, Swansea Town (h) 1-2
1965 – West Bromwich Albion (a) 2-1, Stockport County (h) 1-1 and (a) 2-0, Bolton Wanderers (a) 1-0, Leicester City (a) 0-0 and (h) 1-0, Chelsea (semi-final at Villa Park) 2-0, Leeds United (final at Wembley) 2-1, after extra time
1966 – Chelsea (h) 1-2
1967 – Watford (a) 0-0 and (h) 3-1, Aston Villa (h) 1-0, Everton (a) 0-1
1968 – Bournemouth (a) 0-0 and (h) 4-1, Walsall (a) 0-0 and (h) 5-2, Tottenham Hotspur (a) 1-1 and (h) 2-1, West Bromwich Albion (a) 0-0, (h) 1-1 and (at Maine Road) 1-2
1969 – Doncaster Rovers (h) 2-0, Burnley (h) 2-1, Leicester City (a) 0-0 and (h) 0-1
1970 – Coventry City (a) 1-1 and (h) 3-0, Wrexham (h) 3-1, Leicester City (h) 0-0 and (a) 2-0, Watford (a) 0-1
1971 – Aldershot (h) 1-0, Swansea City (h) 3-0, Southampton (h) 1-0, Tottenham Hotspur (h) 0-0 and (a) 1-0, Everton (semi-final at Old Trafford) 2-1, Arsenal (final at Wembley) 1-2
1972 – Oxford United (a) 3-0, Leeds United (h) 0-0 and (a) 0-2
1973 – Burnley (a) 0-0 and (h) 3-0, Manchester City (h) 0-0 and (a) 0-2
1974 – Doncaster Rovers (h) 2-2 and (a) 2-0, Carlisle United (h) 0-0 and (a) 2-0, Ipswich Town (h) 2-0, Bristol City (a) 1-0, Leicester City (semi-final at Old

Old Trafford) 0-0 and (at Villa Park) 3-1, Newcastle United (final at Wembley) 3-0.

1975 – Stoke City (h) 2-0, Ipswich Town (a) 0-1

1976 – West Ham (a) 2-0, Derby County (a) 0-1

Liverpool League and Championship Record

League Record

Season	*Division*	P	W	D	L	F	A	*Points*	*Position*
1893-4	2	28	22	6	0	77	18	50	1
1894-5	1	30	7	8	15	51	70	22	16
1895-6	2	30	22	2	6	106	32	46	1
1896-7	1	30	12	9	9	46	38	33	5
1897-8	1	30	11	6	13	48	45	28	9
1898-9	1	34	19	5	10	49	33	43	2
1899-1900	1	34	14	5	15	49	45	33	10
1900-1	1	34	19	7	8	59	35	45	1
1901-2	1	34	10	12	12	42	38	32	11
1902-3	1	34	17	4	13	68	49	38	5
1903-4	1	34	9	8	17	49	62	26	17
1904-5	2	34	27	4	3	93	25	58	1
1905-6	1	38	23	5	10	79	46	51	1
1906-7	1	38	13	7	18	64	65	33	15
1907-8	1	38	16	6	16	68	61	38	8
1908-9	1	38	15	6	17	57	65	36	16
1909-10	1	38	21	6	11	78	57	48	2
1910-11	1	38	15	7	16	53	53	37	13
1911-12	1	38	12	10	16	49	55	34	17
1912-13	1	38	16	5	17	61	71	37	12
1913-14	1	38	14	7	17	46	62	35	16
1914-15	1	38	14	9	15	65	75	37	14

FIRST WORLD WAR INTERVENED

Season	*Division*	P	W	D	L	F	A	*Points*	*Position*
1919-20	1	42	19	10	13	59	44	48	4
1920-21	1	42	18	15	9	63	35	51	4
1921-22	1	42	22	13	7	63	36	57	1
1922-23	1	42	26	8	8	70	31	60	1
1923-24	1	42	15	11	16	49	48	41	12
1924-25	1	42	20	10	12	63	55	50	4
1925-26	1	42	14	16	12	70	63	44	7
1926-27	1	42	18	7	17	69	61	43	9
1927-28	1	42	13	13	16	84	87	39	16
1928-29	1	42	17	12	13	90	64	46	5
1929-30	1	42	16	9	17	63	79	41	12
1930-31	1	42	15	12	15	86	85	42	9
1931-32	1	42	19	6	17	81	93	44	10
1932-33	1	42	14	11	17	79	84	39	14
1933-34	1	42	14	10	18	79	87	38	18
1934-35	1	42	19	7	16	85	88	45	7
1935-36	1	42	13	12	17	60	64	38	19
1936-37	1	42	12	11	19	62	84	35	18
1937-38	1	42	15	11	16	65	71	41	11
1938-39	1	42	14	14	14	62	63	42	11
1939-40	1	3	2	0	1	6	3	4	–
	SECOND WORLD WAR INTERVENED								
1946-47	1	42	25	7	10	84	52	57	1
1947-48	1	42	16	10	16	65	61	42	11
1948-49	1	42	13	14	15	53	43	40	12
1949-50	1	42	17	14	11	64	54	48	8
1950-51	1	42	16	11	15	53	59	43	9
1951-52	1	42	12	19	11	57	61	43	11
1952-53	1	42	14	8	20	61	82	36	17
1953-54	1	42	9	10	23	68	97	28	22
1954-55	2	42	16	10	16	92	96	42	11
1955-56	2	42	21	6	15	85	63	48	3
1956-57	2	42	21	11	10	82	54	53	3
1957-58	2	42	22	10	10	79	54	54	4

Season	*Division*	P	W	D	L	F	A	*Points*	*Position*
1958-59	2	42	24	5	13	87	62	53	4
1959-60	2	42	20	10	12	90	66	50	3
1960-61	2	42	21	10	11	87	58	52	3
1961-62	2	42	27	8	7	99	43	62	1
1962-63	1	42	17	10	15	71	59	44	8
1963-64	1	42	26	5	11	92	45	57	1
1964-65	1	42	17	10	15	67	73	44	7
1965-66	1	42	26	9	7	79	34	61	1
1966-67	1	42	19	13	10	64	47	51	5
1967-68	1	42	22	9	11	71	40	55	3
1968-69	1	42	25	6	11	63	24	61	2
1969-70	1	42	20	11	11	65	42	51	5
1970-71	1	42	17	17	8	42	24	51	5
1971-72	1	42	24	9	9	64	30	57	3
1972-73	1	42	25	10	7	72	42	60	1
1973-74	1	42	22	13	7	52	31	57	2
1974-75	1	42	20	11	11	60	39	51	2
1975-76	1	42	23	14	5	66	31	60	1

This is Liverpool's record in European competition, season by season:

Season 1964-65 **EUROPEAN CUP**

17 August, 1964 Reykjavik (a)	5—0	Hunt 2, Wallace 2, Chisnall
14 September, 1964 Reykjavik (h)	6—1	St John 2, Byrne, Stevenson, Hunt, Graham
25 November, 1964 Anderlecht (h)	3—0	Yeats, Hunt, St John
16 December, 1964 Anderlecht (a)	1—0	Hunt
10 Feburary, 1965 Cologne (a)	0—0	
17 March, 1965 Cologne (h)	0—0	
24 March 1965 Cologne (in Rotterdam)	2—2	Hunt, St John
(Liverpool won on toss of disc)		
4 May, 1965 Inter-Milan (h) (semi-final)	3—1	Callaghan, Hunt, St John
12 May, 1965 Inter-Milan (a)	0—3	

Season 1965-66 **EUROPEAN CUP-WINNERS' CUP**

29 September, 1965 Juventus (a)	0–1	
October 13, 1965 Juventus (h)	2–0	Lawler, Strong
1 December, 1965 Standard Liège (h)	3–1	Lawler 2, Thompson
15 December, 1965 Standard Liège (a)	2–1	Hunt, St John
1 March, 1966 Honved (a)	0–0	
8 March, 1966 Honved (h)	2–0	Lawler, St John
14 April, 1966 Glasgow Celtic (a) (semi-final)	0–1	
19 April, 1966 Glasgow Celtic (h)	2–0	Smith, Strong
5 May, 1966 Borussia Dortmund (final in Glasgow)	1–2	Hunt

Season 1966-67 **EUROPEAN CUP**

18 September, 1966 Petrolul Ploesti (h)	2–0	Callaghan, St John
12 October, 1966 Petrolul Ploesti (a)	1–3	Hunt
19 October, 1966 Petrolul Ploesti (in Brussels)	2–0	St John, Thompson
7 December, 1966 Ajax (a)	1–5	Lawler
14 December, 1966 Ajax (h)	2–2	Hunt 2

Season 1967-68 **EUROPEAN FAIRS CUP**

19 September, 1967 Malmo (a)	2–0	Hateley 2
4 October, 1967 Malmo (h)	2–1	Hunt, Yeats
7 November, 1967 Munich 1860 (h)	8–0	Hunt 2, Callaghan 2, Hateley, St John, Thompson, Smith (penalty)
14 November, 1967 Munich 1860 (a)	1–2	Callaghan
28 November, 1967 Ferencvaros (a)	0–1	
1 January, 1968 Ferencvaros (h)	0–1	

Season 1968-69 **EUROPEAN FAIRS CUP**

18 September, 1968 Bilbao (a)	1–2	Hunt
2 October, 1968 Bilbao (h)	2–1	Lawler, Hughes

(Liverpool lost tie on toss of disc)

Season 1969-70 **EUROPEAN FAIRS CUP**

September 16, 1969 Dundalk (h)	10–0	Smith 2, Evans 2, Graham 2, Lawler, Callaghan, Lindsay, Thompson
30 September, 1969 Dundalk (a)	4–0	Thompson 2, Callaghan, Graham
12 November, 1969 Vitoria Setubal (a)	0–1	
26 November, 1969 Vitoria Setubal (h)	3–2	Hunt, Evans, Smith (penalty)

(Liverpool lost, on away goals counting double)

Season 1970-71 **EUROPEAN FAIRS CUP**

15 September, 1970 Ferencvaros (h)	1–0	Graham
29 September, 1970 Ferencvaros (a)	1–1	Hughes
21 October, 1970 Dinamo Bucharest (h)	3–0	Lindsay, Lawler, Hughes
4 November, 1970 Dinamo Bucharest (a)	1–1	Boersma
9 December, 1970 Hibernian (a)	1–0	Toshack
22 December, 1970 Hibernian (h)	2–0	Heighway, Boersma
10 March, 1971 Bayern Munich (h)	3–0	Evans 3
24 March, 1971 Bayern Munich (a)	1–1	Ross
14 April, 1971 Leeds United (h) (semi-final)	0–1	
28 April, 1971 Leeds United (a)	0–0	

Season 1971-72 **EUROPEAN CUP-WINNERS' CUP**

15 September, 1971 Servette Geneva (a)	1–2	Lawler
29 September, 1971 Servette Geneva (h)	2–0	Hughes, Heighway
20 October, 1971 Bayern Munich (h)	0–0	
3 November, 1971 Bayern Munich (a)	1–3	Evans

Season 1972-73 **UEFA CUP**

12 September, 1972 Eintracht Frankfurt (h)	2–0	Keegan, Hughes
26 September, 1972 Eintracht Frankfurt (a)	0–0	
24 October, 1972 A.E.K. Athens (h)	3–0	Smith (penalty), Cormack, Boersma
7 November, 1972 A.E.K. Athens (a)	3–1	Hughes 2, Boersma
29 November, 1972 Dynamo Berlin (a)	0–0	
13 December, 1972 Dynamo Berlin (h)	3–1	Heighway, Toshack, Boersma
7 March, 1973 Dynamo Dresden (h)	2–0	Boersma, Hall

21 March, 1973 Dynamo Dresden (a)	1–0	Keegan
10 April, 1973 Tottenham Hotspur (h) (semi-final)	1–0	Lindsay
25 April, 1973 Tottenham Hotspur (a)	1–2	Heighway
(Liverpool won, on away goals counting double)		
9 May, 1973 Borussian Moenchengladbach (h) (final)	3–0	Keegan 2, Lloyd
23 May, 1973 Borussia Moenchengladbach (a)	0–2	
(Liverpool won UEFA Cup on aggregate victory)		

Season 1973-74 **EUROPEAN CUP**

19 September, 1973 Jeunesse D'Esch (a)	1–1	Hall
3 October, 1973 Jeunesse D'Esch (h)	2–0	Toshack, Mond (own goal)
24 October, 1973 Red Star Belgrade (a)	1–2	Lawler
6 November, 1973 Red Star Belgrade (h)	1–2	Lawler

Season 1974-75 **EUROPEAN CUP-WINNERS' CUP**

17 September, 1974 Stromsgodset (h)	11–0	Lindsay (penalty), Thompson,2, Boersma 2, Heighway, Cormack, Hughes, Smith, Kennedy, Callaghan
1 October, 1974 Stromsgodset (a)	1–0	Kennedy
23 October, 1974 Ferencvaros (h)	1–1	Keegan
5 November, 1974 Ferencvaros (a)	0–0	
(Ferencvaros won on away goals counting double)		

Season 1975-76 **UEFA CUP**

17 September, 1975 Hibernian (a)	0–1	
30 September, 1975 Hibernian (h)	3–1	Toshack 3
22 October, 1975 Real Sociedad (a)	3–1	Heighway, Callaghan, Thompson
4 November, 1975 Real Sociedad (h)	6–0	Toshack, Kennedy 2, Fairclough, Heighway, Neal
26 November, 1975 Slask Wroclaw (a)	2–1	Kennedy, Toshack
10 December, 1975 Slask Wroclaw (h)	3–0	Case 3
3 March, 1976 Dynamo Dresden (a)	0–0	

17 March, 1976 Dynamo Dresden (h)	2–1	Case, Keegan
30 March, 1976 Barcelona (a) (semi-final)	1–0	Toshack
14 April, 1976 Barcelona (h) (semi-final)	1–1	Thompson
28 April, 1976 FC Bruges (h)	3–2	Kennedy, Case, Keegan (penalty)
19 May, 1976 FC Bruges (a) (final)	1–1	Keegan (Liverpool won UEFA Cup on aggregate victory)

LEAGUE CUP RECORD

Season 1960-61: Luton Town (h) 1–1, (a) 5–2; Southampton (h) 1–2
Season 1967-68: Bolton (h) 1–1, (a) 2–3.
Season 1968-69: Sheffield United (h) 4–0, Swansea (h) 2–0, Arsenal (a) 1–2
Season 1969-70: Watford (a) 2–1, Machester City (a) 2–3
Season 1970-71: Mansfield (a) 0–0, (h) 3–2 (after extra time); Swindon (a) 0–2
Season 1971-72: Hull City (h) 3–0, Southampton (h) 1–0, West Ham (a) 1–2
Season 1972-73: Carlisle (a) 1–1, (h) 5–1; West Brom (a) 1–1, (h) 2–1; Leeds United (h) 2–2, (a) 1–0; Tottenham Hotspur (h) 1–1, (a) 1–3.
Season 1973-74: West Ham (a) 2–2, (h) 1–0; Sunderland (a) 2–0; Hull City (a) 0–0, (h) 3–1; Wolves (a) 0–1
Season 1974-75: Brentford (h) 2–1; Bristol City (a) 0–0, (h) 4–0; Middlesbrough (h) 0–1
Season 1975-76: York City (a) 1–0; Burnley (h) 1–1, (a) 0–1